Always Ready

Always Ready

Helping "pre-Christians" understand
how God really forgives

Rev. Ronald A. Hotrum

Ron Hotrum
1Peter 3:15

WESTBOW
P R E S S

A DIVISION OF THOMAS NELSON

ISBN: 978-1-4497-4406-9 (sc)
ISBN: 978-1-4497-4405-2 (e)

WestBow Press books may be ordered through booksellers or by contacting:

WestBow Press
A Division of Thomas Nelson
1663 Liberty Drive
Bloomington, IN 47403
www.westbowpress.com
1-(866) 928-1240

Library of Congress Control Number: 2012905140

Printed in the United States of America

WestBow Press rev. date: 04/30/2012

AUTHOR'S FORWORD

I never was one to pick out a "year verse" as part of a New Year's ritual. Nor have I done that for a "life verse" either. But as I look back over forty years of vocational Christian ministry I can see that the single verse of Scripture that turned out to have been my life verse has been "I am not ashamed of the gospel, because it is the power of God for the salvation of everyone who believes" (Romans 1:16).

People may be ashamed of many different things—their clothes, their lack of education or even the family into which they were born—but think about it, why should any one of us be ashamed of the Gospel? After all, don't we all tend to be proud of something we have that works well and does the job, whether it's a new car, a classic car or even a new lawnmower? I surely wouldn't be ashamed if I had a Ferrari in a Ford neighborhood! Relax, it will never happen, but you do get the point, I am sure.

I learned early that the Gospel as revealed in the Scriptures is the only thing that does all it claims to do. For that reason I've never been ashamed of the Gospel. I have never felt that I needed to because it's always worked. I've been proud to associate myself with something that will last for eternity. That life-altering concept has led to five decades of one-on-one ministry that my wife and others have urged me to write about.

For the past 11 years I have been involved as a chaplain with Nursing Home Ministries, Inc. based in Portland, Oregon. One of my duties was to write a monthly letter letting my financial supporters know what God had been doing during the previous month. Those letters have become thank-you notes, activity reports and prayer requests all in one package. They have been the source of much of the material for this book. I have also drawn upon the records I've kept about people I've prayed with over three decades of pastoral ministry.

During those years as a visiting nursing home chaplain there have been many people who have prayed with me to receive God's forgiveness as a gift and been born into His family, the Church. These stories of new faith are always exciting, aren't they? They have been many but they weren't the first. This kind of thing has been happening to me ever since God called me to a vocation of Christian ministry.

This book will tell that story. I hope it will be both an encouragement and a training tool to help you feel more comfortable following the nudges you get from God now and then to talk with someone about their spiritual needs. Speaking of nudges, let me encourage you to read Bruce Wilkinson's excellent new book, *You Were Born For This*. He uses the term "nudge" to describe how God alerts those who are prepared to help a seeker find the way to forgiveness in Christ. As I read it I realized that what he suggests for Christians to adopt as a habit I had been practicing for decades as the Lord had led. Reading it affirmed to me that I'd been on the right track all along.

This book is an attempt to share my experiences and insights in a way that I hope will be helpful to all Christians who have a deep desire to make an eternal difference for the Kingdom. I don't want to make it seem to anyone that these stories are meant to make me look good or enhance my image, however. I am ever mindful that the ministry of personal evangelism is always built on the efforts of all those who have gone before.

I will let the Apostle Paul speak for me, "What, after all, is Apollos? And what is Paul? Only servants, through whom you came to believe— as the Lord has assigned to each his task. I planted the seed, Apollos watered it, but God made it grow. So neither he who plants nor he who waters is anything, but only God, who makes things grow" (1Corinthians 3:5-9a). Isn't it still true that it is God who makes things grow? Aren't we all just following the Great Commission to make disciples of as many as possible? And aren't we all part of the same team?

I also need to give you a bit of warning at the outset because writing this book as I have planned may seem a bit confusing because I will be doing three things at once. First, because prayer is so essential for the work of bringing individuals to faith in Christ, I will be giving some practical instructions to help our prayers be more effective as we pray for each other as Christians, for the spiritual needs of pre-Christians and for the world's spiritual needs in a way that actually should become an important part of any discipleship effort with new Christians. Without prayer our ministries will tend to become more social work than spiritual work, so I'll focus first on prayer.

As the Spirit anoints us to pray, we actually connect the power of God by faith to those for whom we intercede. God often goes through another person to give a message to someone. We might think of it as intercession that begins with God first, then moves through the one who prays before going on to the target audience. I can think of many examples from Scripture.

When the prophet Samuel was still a young boy he heard a voice calling out to him in the night as he lay sleeping in his room in the tabernacle. That is the part of the story I heard from my Sunday School teachers when I was a child. It was years later that I found out that the important thing that happened that night was not that Samuel was learning to recognize the voice of God. The important thing was the message itself. God came to him with a message that needed to be delivered to the priest, Eli--that Eli and his sons needed to change their ways and seek God's forgiveness. They didn't do that but Samuel got the message and delivered it. That was intercession combined with outreach.

When David wasn't yet feeling the need for God's forgiveness for his sin against Bathsheba and her husband, God spoke to the prophet Nathan who was then instructed to take the message to the king. The result was David falling on his face before God to beg forgiveness for his sins of adultery and murder. Nathan became an intercessor for the Lord—he was the go-between.

When Naaman, the Syrian army commander wanted to be healed of his leprosy it was the intercession of his servant girl who brought God's message to him about the steps he needed to take to get help. The result was his decision to travel all the way to Israel to look up Elisha, a prophet of God, to be healed. But the cure was unthinkable—he had to immerse himself in the muddy waters of the Jordan River trusting that the God of Israel would heal him. Naaman's servant girl was the intercessor.

And finally, when Saul of Tarsus was on his murderous rampage arresting Christians in the capitol city of a foreign country, he was interrupted by the Lord Jesus as he came near Damascus. It was God's voice to Ananias, a believer in that city, which made the difference. God's instructions were for Ananias to go meet Saul, to anoint him and to pray for him to be released and forgiven. The result in Saul's case was the salvation of the man who would later do more to spread the Gospel of Christ than any of Jesus' original twelve apostles. Can you see how Ananias was an intercessor—a go-between who stood between God and Saul?

Have you ever wondered why God didn't just deliver the messages Himself directly? What benefit could possibly have come from involving an uninterested third party? Think of how terrifying it must have been for any of these intercessors. None wanted to approach someone who had the power to make his life miserable or even to take his life.

I think that may be the point. It moves the uninterested bystanders to take part; it gets more people involved in Kingdom business. Evangelism and intercession must go together because that's the way God has always worked. He lets us in on the activity as we partner with Him to reach others. Here is the Bible's encouragement to us: "If anyone sees his brother sin a sin which is not unto death, let him pray and God will give him life" (1 John 5:16).

Through prayer we are actually making connections between God and those who are still on the way to knowing Him as Savior. I think that you will agree with me that because we all have benefited from the intercessory prayers of others we have an obligation to intercede with our heavenly Father for the spiritual needs of those around us.

Here's an example from our family. It has become a frequently repeated account of how my wife's father came to personal faith in Christ. Gloria, Janice's mother, was a Christian who regularly attended a great church. Earl, her father, was a generous and thoughtful man in many ways but was totally uninterested in spiritual things. He chose not to be involved in any way and made it plain that his decision was final. Because he didn't have a son who could grow up to be a drinking buddy he was very disappointed when she married me--a guy who made it plain that he was in training to become a pastor. Now he wouldn't even have a son-in-law who would fill that role. Earl did attend church most Christmas mornings with the family, however, and later when I was pastoring he would occasionally attend where we were pastoring.

As the years went by and our three sons came along, we trained them to pray that Grampa would realize how much he needed to be forgiven and come to faith in Christ. They learned to pray early and often that Grampa would accept God's gracious gift of being born again and that the Holy Spirit would surround him until he did.

Later we moved away from the Portland area where Janice's folks lived so we only saw them about twice a year. Each time we came to visit for a few days it was up to me, of course, to offer the prayer of thanks for the meals. More years went by with our sons still praying for Grampa until he became sick with the disease that would take his life when he was only 64.

With the news that Grampa's illness was getting worse we made the 360 mile trip to Portland more frequently to see him. One day Janice got a call from her dad wanting to know when we would be coming again. He said that he had a surprise for us. We arranged to come in about two weeks and when we arrived we received the shock of our lives. As we sat down to the supper table Earl said, "Ron, all these years you have been saying grace before meals. Now it's finally my turn. I've given my heart to the Lord." I will have to admit that we were left more speechless than believing.

Now for the *rest of the story*, as the radio commentator Paul Harvey used to say. Janice had contacted Steve, her mother's pastor, asking him to go see Earl in the hospital to see if he would be willing to talk with him about his need for the Lord. Earl had rebuffed similar efforts from all of us over the years and even now over the months of his severe illness as well. Dutifully, Pastor Steve went to see Earl one more time only to be turned away once again.

When the pastor got to the elevator he pushed the button for the lobby. While he waited for the elevator to come, the Lord just seemed to speak clearly to him, "Go back and talk to Earl one more time." Reluctantly and fearfully, but obediently, he returned to Earl's room to hear him say as he entered, "I was hoping you would come back." I am sure you can believe that because Earl was finally really ready he quickly prayed to receive God's forgiveness as a gift of His grace! Can you also believe that our family has thanked God many times over the years for the way that Gloria's pastor was alert to God's voice, bold to speak for Jesus, as compassionate as Jesus who looked on the multitudes as sheep without a shepherd, discerning into the needs of a pre-Christian and endured until the victory was won! In Chapter Four you will see these same five characteristics become part of a planned prayer focus.

What a joy for our family to see the results of frequent, fervent prayer for the salvation of a loved one by praying that he would feel the need for God's forgiveness. How excited Janice and I were the next morning to see Earl and Gloria reading the Bible together before breakfast. When he died just a few weeks later I was able to joyfully tell Earl's story at the memorial that was well attended because of his years of holding positions of leadership in two large organizations in Portland—the Elks and the American Legion, Post 1. His drinking buddies were all there to hear the story of Earl's most important decision as Pastor Steve and I shared in the service.

This family experience has also confirmed my conviction that God just loves to answer the prayers of children. If you want to see a loved one come to the end of themselves and the beginning of a faith relationship with Christ, I suggest that you get some sincere Christian children to agree in prayer. I do believe God wants to answer their prayers if for no other reason than to build their faith. Remember the words of Scripture: "He is patient with you, not wanting anyone to perish, but everyone to come to repentance" (2 Peter 3:9). Since we know it's God's will we can pray in faith. That doesn't mean, of course, that everyone will come to Christ but it does mean that we will always be in line with God's will as we do pray.

Second, I will also give some instructions about the necessary truths "pre-Christians" need to understand in order to come to faith in Christ. I will start that process by exposing the mistaken notions that many pre-

Christians have of how God forgives to the light of Scriptural truths. It will become plainer later, trust me.

And third, I will intersperse dozens of examples of people who have come from confusion to understanding, from cynic to seeker and from seeker to salvation through the whole process. Whenever I share the stories of people I've encountered, either I will not use their names at all or the names will be changed unless otherwise indicated. The accounts will remain factual, however.

Just to be clear, the term "pre-Christian" is surely not new with me. I join others in using it to communicate the truth that there are really only two kinds of people in this world: Christians, and those who aren't Christians yet. Those who are still on the way I call "pre-Christians." That, of course, doesn't mean that all will eventually come to personal faith in Christ. It almost means the opposite. Unless a person does come to personal faith in Christ through confession of sin, repentance from sin and surrender to Christ as Lord, he isn't a Christian. He is still on the outside, still on the way. Isn't that one of the underlying truths of the New Testament, "If we confess our sins, he is faithful and just and will forgive us our sins and purify us from all unrighteousness" (1 John 1:9)?

As I look back over my own life I am sure I was on the way long before I realized it. I also knew in my heart that I was still on the outside looking in but wanting to be on the inside looking out. That discussion will be included in chapter two.

Rev. Ronald A. Hotrum
2012

ACKNOWLEDGEMENTS

I am deeply grateful to Janice, my wife of over forty five years, who has been my closest confidante and ministry partner, and to Brian, our pastor-son who returned the favor of offering many suggestions and corrections to this manuscript as I did for him on his book a few years ago. This project would not have been possible without their helpful suggestions and encouragement.

I also am indebted to Dr. John F. Sills, General Superintendent Emeritus of the Evangelical Church; Dr. J. Dale Erbele, Director of Harvest Ministries of the Evangelical Church; Rev. Donald A. DeBoer, Executive Director of Nursing Home Ministries, Inc. and Dr. Robert L. Morris, Professor, Bethel College, Mishawaka, Indiana. Each of these men gave valuable suggestions which helped make the book better than it would have been without their time and efforts.

CONTENTS

1

A SCRIPTURAL COMMAND

Before I tell my own story, I need you to look with me at the Scriptural key to this book: "But in your hearts set apart Christ as Lord. Always be prepared to give an answer to everyone who asks you to give the reason for the hope that you have. But do this with gentleness and respect, keeping a clear conscience" (1 Peter 3:15-16a). Notice with me the five simple but essential steps that appear in this passage.

First is to set Christ apart as absolute Lord in our lives. This may be the greatest hindrance most Christians encounter in their efforts to share their faith with other people. They themselves have areas of life that have yet to be yielded to the control of Christ. They may have received God's forgiveness and have experienced the new birth, but they have not yet seen that their spiritual needs go much deeper. The old truism which says "If Christ isn't Lord of all He isn't Lord at all" is still true. That subject is treated well by others so I won't dwell on it. My purpose here is just to note it and also have you notice that it comes first in order and therefore first in priority. If you are facing personal spiritual struggles in allowing Christ to be absolute Lord of your life, find a trusted Christian friend to pray with you as you come to the end of yourself. Set apart Christ as Lord.

Second, Peter says we are always to be prepared to give an answer to anyone who asks why we know we are headed for heaven. Did you notice that this is a command and not simply a suggestion? Later we

1

will talk about *how* to prepare. Suffice it to say here that the obligation is upon us to get prepared and stay alert for seekers. I firmly believe that the Lord will bring seekers to those who are ready. So let's get ready, stay ready, hone our skills and be alert for pre-Christians who are already seekers.

Third, the answer itself is our focus. While different people have different emotional, mental and psychosocial needs, and it is good for us to minister to the whole person, pre-Christians all share the one need of receiving God's forgiveness through faith in Christ. That's the only need that if unmet will have eternal consequences. Peter wants us to focus primarily on *that* need.

Fourth, we are to focus specifically on the "reason for the hope that you have." If we have no hope we have nothing to share and no one will be interested. Do keep in mind that the Bible tends to use the word "hope" more as a noun than a verb. Our culture has used the word "hope" as a verb to express a personal preference: "I sure hope it doesn't rain on parade day." The Bible speaks of hope as a noun, a thing promised and paid for but still pending. One might say, "Signed, sealed but not yet delivered." A good example would be "Christ in you, the hope of glory" (Colossians 1:27). That hope is always linked to eternal life with Christ starting now and continuing on into eternity. That hope is not based on mere preference. It has a *reason*. That's what Peter wants us to focus on here. Why is putting our confidence in Christ a reasonable thing to do? We'll cover the answer to that much more in detail in chapter five.

Fifth, "give your answer with gentleness and respect; never violate your conscience." These character traits are once again not optional since Peter lists them as requirements. This may take some thoughtful decision making on our parts before we open our mouths to talk about our confidence in the Lord. We will certainly need to think about how we may answer a person who is being rude. But we can always plan to be gentle and respectful, I'm sure.

Christians effectively sharing the story of their faith journey will be aware of what not to say, too. Being bold doesn't have to mean being brash, does it? When we lack gentleness and respect for other people we can too easily get into arguments about peripheral doctrinal points. Do you think anyone was ever argued into the Kingdom? I don't either. You may win the argument but you will most likely also lose further opportunities to win that person for Christ.

Let me give you an example. In one of my facilities I met a man for the first time, introduced myself as the company chaplain and asked if he had anyone to come visit him while he was there. (Those are my traditional "opening lines.") As we chatted awhile I said, "Isn't it good to know that God loves us?" That seemed to be okay with him so I went on talking about spiritual things, arriving soon at one of my favorite questions learned in "Evangelism Explosion" training some forty years ago: "Have you come to the place in your spiritual life where you know for absolute certainty that when you die you will go to heaven to be with Jesus?" His unique response floored me, "Not necessary for me to answer that; it does not apply to me." When I asked him why, he replied that it was because he wasn't going to die, he simply refused to die so it wouldn't be an issue. No amount of gently trying to guide the conversation moved him away from that position so I had to let it go. Later I'll share more about how to keep the discussion on track.

2

MY OWN STORY

I had many advantages as a young child. Because my maternal grandfather was a pastor we attended church regularly. I recall that when we visited their home there was a time of family worship right after breakfast, as well. Grampa could also be heard humming hymns and gospel songs under his breath as he puttered around in his shop. One of his favorites must have been *Revive Us Again* because I remember hearing that a lot. God used all of that and more to begin to open my heart to Him.

Because I felt the need for God's forgiveness early in life I prayed earnestly and often to receive it. But it wasn't until I was a high school student at church youth camp in late August of 1961 that I finally found peace with God. I was fifteen years old. To this day I distinctly remember the experience of realizing that God's forgiveness was a gift that could only be received like any other gift. I clearly recall running from the chapel back to our church's cabin to tell someone of my new-found peace with God. Finding my Aunt Marion there working in the kitchen, I burst out, "It's just as easy as falling off a log!" I have never forgotten those words and that new level of faith.

For the first time I had truly fallen backwards onto the Lord as an act of faith in Him alone, knowing that my sins were forgiven and I was now a child of God. For me that experience also coincided with answering God's call on my life to be a minister. I didn't know

5

what forms that calling might take; I was totally willing to accept any assignment. I was so moved that when I went back to school a few weeks later I changed some of the courses in my semester schedule. I moved away from additional math, science and architectural drawing to speech, music, vocabulary and foreign languages.

Even then I also sensed that God was blessing me with the gifts to serve as an evangelist. I became a leader in my high school's Youth for Christ Club, taught Bible studies and joined with others in raising the necessary funds so we could show films produced by the Billy Graham Evangelistic Association in our high school auditorium after school. I'll share later how my boldness earned me a visit to the Vice Principal's office. But despite such setbacks we were seeing some of our friends come to faith in Christ.

I also remember that there were times when the Lord put such a burden on my heart for lost people that at the close of a service at the church where our family attended I walked up to the platform, gained permission from the pastor to speak and after extending an invitation for fellow members of the youth group to make a total surrender to the Lord I saw many come forward to pray and they received help for their spiritual needs. I distinctly remember one occasion when there were ten of us high school kids responding together at one time to give ourselves to lives of ministry should God so choose to call us. I was seeing God work through me in unexpected ways and realized that these were *God moments.*

In order to receive Bible training for ministry I attended Cascade College in Portland, Oregon, which was a big move for a farm boy from Spokane, Washington. Once again my Cleveland grandparents helped out in many ways to make it possible. They moved to the campus and began to work in the school book store so I would be spared the expenses of staying in the dorm and eating in the cafeteria.

During my first week of school I began to get acquainted with Janice Glasscock, who would later become my wife. When I discovered that she, too, was involved in ministry already, I knew I had found a kindred spirit. She had been teaching children's Bible clubs during her high school years, too. We got married and both of us were able to finish college. She went on to teaching and I went on to Western Evangelical Seminary for more training.

During my seminary years I became the youth pastor at a downtown church that was located just a few blocks from the marching route of the annual Portland Rose Festival Parade. Knowing that the world would literally be marching right past our church door, I had been training the high school students in my youth group how to use the Four Spiritual Laws booklets provided by Campus Crusade for Christ.

On parade day I stayed about twenty feet behind the actual parade route, sitting on a curb in the park, looking for someone to visit with. As I sat there I looked down and there scratched into the cement when it had still been soft were these words, "Time is brought to you by the Maker of space." Some philosophy student from nearby Portland State University must have left his mark. Those words soon became a discussion starter and I was able to present the Gospel message to a young man that day.

In 1971 after three years of seminary training, I was ordained as an elder in the Evangelical Church and received my first assignment in full time ministry at the Manor Evangelical Church in Clark County, Washington. I had just turned twenty five.

Feeling the need for more training in evangelism and after exploring many options, I chose to attend the "Evangelism Explosion" training that was offered in nearby Portland, Oregon. That training gave me the tools I needed to get a good start for these past forty years of ministry as a personal evangelist, a pastor, a camp speaker and a nursing home chaplain.

I've spent these forty years refining the presentation, sharpening the tools and using them in many applications. During that time I have watched God at work as I've prayed with over two hundred people in one-on-one situations plus many other experiences as an altar worker at church camps. It is from these experiences that I'll be sharing throughout this volume. But first we must do some training in effective prayer methods.

Prayer is like plowing—absolutely necessary for preparing the seedbed before planting. But too often our prayers are so unfocused as to be nearly unanswerable. In that regard praying is like aiming a hunting rifle before pulling the trigger. Surely one would expect to be a more successful hunter that way than just by occasionally firing into the air or into the woods just hoping to hit something edible. So let me teach you a focusing tool for your prayer life.

3

PRAYER AS PREPARATION

As I mentioned earlier, prayer is the first focus of this book. Remember, prayer is like plowing—both are essential to preparing the soil for the seed. I'm going to assume that you are in full agreement and you are already setting aside time for private worship and intercession every day. But, once again, if you find yourself struggling in this area of your spiritual life, take the opportunity to set new priorities and schedules to make prayer in its many forms a vital part of your life. My wife and I remember well the time we made the decision to just set the alarm to come on earlier in the morning so we could give adequate time for prayer and private worship. Setting new priorities cannot change our lives until we also set new schedules.

You may have tried to make prayer a more important part of your life but your prayers still remained unfocused and you may have found your mind wandering while in private prayer. But let's be honest; you may have had similar problems in times of corporate prayer, too. Have you sat in prayer meetings and noticed the lack of focus as you listened to people pray? Have you been frustrated as you sensed the repetitive nature of so many prayers? Have you even caught *yourself* praying, "God, be *with* so-and-so" and later wondered just what that was supposed to mean? Have you wondered what it was that you expected God to actually *do* when you asked Him to be with someone?

Well, so have I—all of those things. That's why years ago I began to develop and use an easily remembered tool for making my prayer life more of a smorgasbord and less of a meat loaf—that is, having different flavors wherever you slice it than always being the same anywhere you interrupt it. These chapters on prayer are the result of those efforts. I hope they help many more fellow Christians to add flavor and effectiveness to their prayer lives—both private and corporate.

For ease of memory it's based on the alphabet, since that's about the first thing we're taught as children. There are five items in each section since five is a "handful" and is a quantity easy to remember as well. There are three sections, reflecting our circles of influence, like the circles of outreach listed in Acts 1:8 as Jerusalem, Judea and Samaria and finally the ends of the earth. Each of these fifteen topics also comes right out of the Scriptures.

You will notice as we go along that these fifteen topics are all very specific. How many times have you caught yourself merely praying for "God's will to be done" without any reference to His will that is already revealed in the Scriptures! Let me suggest that we make an effort to locate His will and then pray it into practice! These fifteen specific prayer targets also only refer to spiritual needs. Too much time is already given in our prayers for the "organ recital" of each others physical needs and hospital stays. Not that they are unimportant, but just *less* important, wouldn't you agree? Appendix three will cover others areas of prayer and intercession.

I am under no illusion that this is the last word on the subject of index praying. I just offer it as a way that has benefited many people who pray and many more who are prayed for. After all, Jesus himself gave the first index prayer in what we now refer to as the Lord's Prayer. It was a list of subjects formed for ease of memory. My observation, however, is that over the years many people have just used that outline as a substitute for real prayer—real contact with our Heavenly Father. They simply recite the outline and act as if they had just prayed.

Now I suppose that my humble suggestion can be susceptible to the same misuse, but I truly doubt that many people will simply recite the alphabet from A through O and think they have prayed. Give this simple plan a try. See if this is a help to your own prayer life. I've recommended it for years; I have used it for years and have had no warranty calls yet!

I believe it so much that whenever possible I'll have Janice pray specifically during a "Salvation Appointment" I may have with a person. She will pray specifically for my needs and for their needs. When I return I'll report the results to her. As I work my way along through these prayer topics I'll intersperse them with anecdotes of my encounters with seekers.

4

CHRISTIANS PRAYING FOR EACH OTHER

The first five letters of the alphabet can remind us of five spiritual character traits we need as Christians if we are to be effective in ministry: Alertness to God's voice, Boldness for Christ before the world, the Compassion of Christ for people around us, Discernment into the needs of others as well as to see the tricks of Satan as he tries to derail our lives and finally, Endurance.

ALERTNESS TO GOD:

I grew up in the church and enjoyed it. I already told you how I experienced the new birth over fifty years ago as a high school student. One of the earliest memories I have of an encounter with the Lord after that was while sitting in the back row of our little stone church (That's where the cool teens sat during the early 60's. Has anything really changed?)

I remember having an overwhelming desire for God's Spirit to always keep me sensitive to Him by keeping me alert to His voice. As tears eased off my trembling chin onto my hands I silently prayed, "God, never let me lose this sense of newness. Keep me alert to your voice!

When you speak I want to be able to hear. And if that means that some may think that I'm just a cry-baby, so be it."

I guess I had noticed that some older Christians may have lost their edge, so to speak. Maybe I was a bit judgmental then, but I'm still praying for a fresh alertness to God and you probably are, too, when you think about it.

One occasion that forcefully brought this home to me again was a remark my Grandpa Cleveland made when he was at our house for his 90th birthday celebration. It was nearly a decade ago now that we were sitting together on the sofa while others were mingling and visiting. He had been the example I looked up to in a person who was always listening to God's voice and following through on what He said.

I already knew that every day when the mail truck came to their mobile home park he would look to see when there would be a crowd of residents around the mailbox row and that's when he would "make his move," heading out to talk to people about Jesus. He leaned over to me and said, "Ronnie, this past year has been the best year of my life spiritually. I feel like I've grown closer to God more this year than ever before." Once again, I was reminded of how far I have to go in this endeavor and the necessity of making every effort to remain alert to God's voice.

Now let me draw your attention to some Scriptural examples that make mention of this fundamental necessity for maintaining an alertness to God's voice. There's Samuel, of course, who learned as a child to reply, "Speak, for your servant is listening" (I Samuel 3:10). There was Elijah who had to quit being impressed by the earthquake, wind and fire and get quiet enough to hear God speak as a "gentle whisper" (I Kings 19:12). Even Jesus, toward the end of His earthly ministry told His disciples "I do nothing on my own but speak just what the Father has taught me" (John 8:28). As a result "All the people hung on his words." (Luke 19:48). So if we are going to follow the example of our Lord, alertness to the Father is the first thing we need.

I believe He wants us to ask for it because He only gives it when we do ask. It seems to work best that way for me, anyway. As I approach a building or a person I frequently find myself asking God for this continued level of sensitivity to Him so I won't miss out on ministry assignments for that day. Many times He has instantly reminded me of a particular person He wants me to be sure to see in that building.

"Allen" was one of those. His wife, a wonderful Christian lady, was a resident in one of my buildings when I met him. We got acquainted over the next few weeks and soon began to talk about spiritual things. He was a retired outside salesmen for a company dealing with medical equipment. He was short, well groomed, had a pleasant smile and his gray hair was combed straight back. He was always well dressed and was there for his wife nearly every day.

As it happened, I didn't see him for a few weeks. When I entered that building one Monday morning the Lord just seemed to remind me to go straight to her room and there he was, ready to talk. We subsequently had many good conversations regarding his walk with the Lord. Sad to say, I wasn't able to get through the superficial layers down to eternal assurances before I was laid off by the company. But I'm confident that Gospel seeds were planted and I still pray for him to respond.

How do I pray more specifically for a pre-Christian like that? I'll cover that in the next chapter. Do keep reading; I will cover that in the next chapter.

BOLDNESS:

The second area of life I can see the need to pray for is boldness. Isn't it interesting that the record in Acts 4 shows that these early Christians—perhaps the boldest the world has seen—prayed for yet more boldness! They were the ones who had seen Jesus horribly beaten and executed in the public square and they had every expectation that the save treatment awaited them. But since the outpouring of the Holy Spirit on them on that first Pentecost day they were different people-- their boldness was evident to all. Peter and John had told the arresting officers, "We cannot help speaking about what we have seen and heard" (Acts 4:20). I would call that boldness more than sufficient for the needs at hand! But how did they pray when they were allowed to get together

15

again? "Now, Lord, consider their threats and enable your servants to speak your word with great boldness" (Acts 4:29). The only conclusion we can come to is to follow their example, isn't it?

As I pray for myself and my Christian friends I say, "Lord, give me the boldness that comes with knowing who we are in you--boldness to give clear testimony to a wondering world of what it's like to be your child." Wouldn't you agree that the lack of boldness too often characterizes many Christians today? Have you ever felt paralyzed by unfounded fears? Have you ever felt the need for more boldness? Then let's pray for ourselves and each other to receive this much needed gift from the Lord.

I encourage you to also pray along with the writer to the Hebrews that we would have greater "confidence to enter the Most Holy Place by the blood of Jesus" (Hebrews 10:19). That doesn't mean brashness, of course, but a calm confidence. We need that if we're going to be able to have boldness before the world. Jesus' brother James was right when he wrote "you do not have because you do not ask God" (James 4:2). That is why I tend to believe that our Heavenly Father may be a bit disappointed when we come to Him timidly and so proud of us when we come boldly to ask for more and greater boldness in ministry.

Let me give you an example from my own experience. I went to school during the early sixties when Youth for Christ Clubs were in nearly every large high school. While I was giving leadership to our local chapter we raised the necessary funds to rent current outreach films produced by the Billy Graham Evangelistic Association. We then rented our high school's auditorium, made flyers and went to work publicizing when the next showing would be. I thought the most efficient way to accomplish that task was to go from room to room during the first twenty minutes of the school day while everyone was in their homeroom for announcements anyway. So I set to work.

I got through about four rooms one morning when I was interrupted by a messenger from the Vice Principal's office inviting me to attend a private meeting with the man himself! When I arrived in his office, Mr. D. forcefully explained that what I was doing was not acceptable practice in his school. He explained that I would have to find some other way to get the word out. I'm not sure if it was because this was my first offense or because of my winsome smile but all I know is that I was spared any detention hours or suspension days. I did get the message, however.

As for my response, I led my group to gladly comply with his wishes but also to pray for greater boldness. We were still being bold as we made personal invitations but we didn't need to be brash when dealing with the "brass." I was learning to willingly suffer the consequences of authority while maintaining boldness before my fellow students.

Another example from my own experience is when I was in my mid-thirties. I had left the pastorate to teach full time at a large Christian school for a few years. That freed up my Sundays and soon I was asked to be an interim pastor at a church that had just had their pastor leave under a cloud. The church leaders were also facing another situation with an elder that would require an action of church discipline. On my way across town to my first Sunday there I began to panic.

What would people think of me, so young, trying to grab hold of a difficult situation? Their board of elders was made up of folks plenty older than I was at the time. It got so bad that I felt the Lord directing me to pull the car over. I think we both were feeling the need for a chat. He reminded me that everyone thinks those same thoughts: "What will people think of me?" And since that's the case there would not be anyone else left over to think about me, they would all be thinking about themselves, too. What I needed was that perspective so I could ask Him for the boldness needed to minister. I asked Him for it and I felt Him giving it as I sat there in my car. I arrived and had a great Sunday followed by a board meeting and many months of ministry to follow. That gift of boldness from the Lord was absolutely essential to continued ministry.

But boldness can be misinterpreted—even misused—without compassion. Boldness without compassion is arrogant harshness and compassion without boldness is mere sentimentality. We do need both, don't we?

COMPASSION:

How many times it was noted of Jesus that "He had compassion on them because they were like sheep without a shepherd" (Mark 6:34)? Think, too, of the time when the leprous man came for healing and Jesus reached out a hand of compassion and touched him when touching such a person was both illegal and ill advised. Or the time when the disciples wanted to send the hungry multitudes away but Jesus insisted on feeding them—all 5,000 men, plus women and children!

"O Lord, give us eyes of compassion, as we view the world and its people!" Wasn't that what Peter was urging on his friends when he reminisced about his days with Jesus and then later said, "Finally, all of you, live in harmony with one another; be sympathetic, love as brothers, be compassionate and humble" (1 Peter 3:8).

How many times do we all too easily slip into the old mold of the world and "use people to get things" instead of "using things to gain people for the Kingdom." May God help us to focus on people with the genuine love of Christ, to be redemptive in our hearts as well as by our actions. What a pity it would be if we were merely to minister as if we were just "delivering the mail," so to speak. Without God's character working its way in us we are "only a resounding gong or a clanging cymbal" (1 Corinthians 13:1). And where are we going to get that compassion? From him, of course.

Trust me, there have been times in these years of ministry when I have suffered from "compassion fatigue," when I was tired of dealing with people with so many problems and so few problem-solving skills. But those were also times when I could sense the Lord reminding me that he is still the source for everything I needed. But I had to admit my need of renewed compassion; I needed to ask Jesus for his kind of compassion before I went on. Have I got it down perfectly? Not even close, but at least I know where to go for more when I need it.

DISCERNMENT:

The fourth item in this first handful of prayer targets is discernment. It was James, our Lord's brother, who instructed, "If any of you lacks wisdom, he should ask God who gives generously to all without finding fault, and it will be given to him" (James 1:5).

To begin with, we surely need discernment into the needs of those around us as we pray for them and pray with them and try to minister to them. In my own life I have discovered that concentrating on people I meet with an eye to discovering what God wants for them keeps me from either ignoring them or taking advantage of them. Doing this reminds me that since I'm on God's team, that person I am encountering is either a fellow team member or a prospective team member so I can't ignore them and surely wouldn't want to take advantage of one of God's prospective team members.

Let me give you an example of needing discernment without much notice. I was in one of my buildings working my way down the hall introducing myself to the "newbies" when I met a man whose first question when he found out I was a chaplain was, "Chaplain, I was born a Catholic, and still am, but I have been a member of the Masonic Lodge all my adult life. Can I still be a good Catholic?" His pronounced Boston accent suggested that he came by his Catholic faith not so much from a personal decision as from his Irish family tradition.

He was such a likeable guy I just couldn't help appreciating his forthrightness and openness but I immediately felt like Nehemiah of old who prayed to the Lord of Heaven even as he opened his mouth to give an answer to his King. I sent up a quick prayer asking God how to answer this difficult question. I didn't want to alienate him. It looked like a "lose-lose" situation at first as I tried to figure out how he would respond to any of my possible replies.

Then God just seemed to say, "Ron, think about it. That's not what he really wants to know. He really wants to know if he can know Me." So I said, "I'm wondering if what you really want to know is how you can know God regardless of your past associations and decisions?" His face brightened as he agreed. I asked him if I could take a few minutes to explain to him how he could know God personally.

In later chapters I'll share more specifically what I explained to him, but suffice it to say here that in just a few minutes he confessed his sin through tears, received God's forgiveness with immediate freedom and joy and couldn't wait to call his sister in Boston. As I walked down his hall later that morning he was quick to let me know that he had indeed called his sister. When someone does that you're confident his repentance and confession were both genuine. That's how discernment from God works. It is a *God thing*.

Isn't that how Jesus responded when He was asked by the woman at the well where the right place to worship was? She wanted to make sure she was doing things the right way and when she figured out that she had a prophet on her hands because of the way he knew all about her past she blurted it out. It's almost as if she'd been waiting a long time for this very opportunity. "'Sir,' the woman said, 'I can see that you are a prophet. Our fathers worshiped on this mountain, but you Jews claim that the place where we must worship is in Jerusalem'" (John 4:19).

She asked a question about the right way to do something religious and expected a reply. But can you see how Jesus was presented with only two options? The answer would be either here or there. He wisely did not take the bait. He thoughtfully spoke to her real need when He said, "God is Spirit and those who worship Him must worship him in Spirit and in truth" (John 4:24). How many times people get so concerned about doing things the right way that they forget about making sure they are doing the right things. That will take discernment, won't it?

We will also continually need discernment from God to guide our own lives, too, won't we? Praying for discernment in this area will tend to keep us from viewing the Bible as just another recipe book. We will more likely be tuned into cooperating with God's efforts at developing our Christian character. Praying for discernment into our own spiritual needs is a lot like using the Bible as a mirror that we intentionally hold up so we can find our faults and correct them.

The third area of discernment is for us to be wise to the trickery of the Devil as he would seek to confuse, discourage and tempt us. Jesus told His disciples that He wanted them to "be as shrewd as snakes and as innocent as doves" (Matthew 10:16).

James also informs us of the differences between the wisdom that is from above and that which is from below, "But the wisdom that comes from heaven is first of all pure; then peace-loving, considerate, submissive, full of mercy and good fruit, impartial and sincere" (James 3:17). Surely as we pray this way for ourselves and each other we will be better able to avoid the devil's pitfalls. But of what use is discernment if we quit before we're done? We also need endurance, don't we?

ENDURANCE:

Wasn't it Jesus who told his disciples, "the love of most will grow cold but he who stands firm to the end will be saved" (Matthew 24:13)? You may also recall that He is also the One who said, "Whoever acknowledges me before men, I will also acknowledge him before my Father in heaven, but whoever disowns me before men, I will disown him before my Father in heaven" (Matthew 10:32, 33). As I pray for myself and my Christian friends, I ask that God would grant us whatever perspective is necessary to motivate us to endure. The more we see things in this world through the prism of God's perspective the more likely we are to be people of endurance.

How many times the Apostle Paul urged his friends on in this way: "Let us not become weary in doing good" (Galatians 6:9); "As for you, brothers, never tire of doing what is right" (2 Thessalonians 3:13); "Endure hardship with us like a good soldier of Christ Jesus" (2 Timothy 2:3); and my favorite, "Let nothing move you, always give yourselves fully to the work of the Lord, because you know that your labor in the Lord is not in vain" (1 Corinthians 15:58).

That last verse proves that God will make it worth my while, so to speak, for me to be a Christian of endurance. That's why whether I'm falling asleep at night or falling awake in the morning I pray that we would all be Christians of endurance. In fact, many times I'll be praying through these five topics in intercessory prayer for myself, my wife and our three sons, other members of our extended family or friends at

21

church as I'm lying in bed and be interrupted by sleep, only to wake up later and find myself continuing along the same lines in prayer. I recommend it to you, too.

Once again, have I perfected endurance? Not really, but I have learned that when I am spiritually winded, ready to fold and have hit the wall (which I've done before), I know it's time to realize that this is a spiritual need God can meet.

So here's how a sample prayer might progress from A through E. I'll use myself as an example as I daily prayed for my wife on her way to work before she retired.

"Heavenly Father, as Janice goes to work today I ask that you would continue to give her supernatural **alertness** to your inner promptings--those *heart whispers* from your heart to hers. May her internal spiritual radar be on high alert today as she teaches school. Help her to immediately be able to notice when you might need to give her a mid-course correction during the day. I also pray that today she will be both **bold** to stand in your presence to seek direction and **bold** to stand for you in others' presence as she gives the directions she receives from you. As she does that, may you fill her with the **compassion** of Jesus for all those who will watch her today. Grant this request so that no one will get the wrong idea of what you are like by anything she does or says today. Give her **discernment**, too, into the needs of those around her so that in your hands she'll be the best tool that she can be, and **discernment** into the deceptive ways the devil has of sidetracking us through discouragement, distraction or depression. And finally, may she possess the physical, emotional and spiritual **endurance** necessary to fulfill your will for her and all of those whose lives she will touch today, in the name of Jesus I pray, amen.

I still pray daily for myself and others this same way. Can you see how you could use this prayer outline in many different applications? Can you see how focusing your prayers in this way will be so much more effective that our tasteless requests for God to merely be "with" someone? I hope so. Give it a try and watch for the appropriate answers. They will come; you will see.

22

5

PRAYING FOR PRE-CHRISTIANS & ACCOUNTS OF GOSPEL PRESENTATIONS

As we continue on now to the second handful of ways to pray, I will focus on praying for our *pre-Christian* friends and acquaintances. That's an expression I prefer to the term *non-Christians*. The former is more hopeful, forward looking, a statement of faith in what's possible, don't you think? The term non-Christian makes it sound as if there is no hope for them to be able to make the next step of moving from one group to another. As long as a person can respond to Christ in faith, confession and repentance there is hope and there will be forgiveness, life and new birth. (See the Author's Forward for a fuller discussion of this topic.)

Let's go on now to topics "F" through "J". As we work through the next five topics for prayer you will see that these are five areas of spiritual need and understanding that pre-Christians need to address before they will turn in full surrender to Christ as Savior. They are: coming to the place where they Feel the need for God's Forgiveness, understanding the concept of God's Grace that makes forgiveness a Gift, having the Holy

Spirit remove the spiritual Hindrances in their lives, being willing to Ignore the Idols in their lives and finally, understanding that Judgment for sin is sure and certain unless they accept God's forgiveness.

This chapter may seem to be a bit disjointed because I am going to combine three things together as we go along: topics for prayer for our pre-Christian friends, an outline of how I explain the necessary truths of the gospel to seekers along with examples of many people who have actually experienced this. Let's give it a try.

FEEL THE NEED FOR FORGIVENESS:

Do you remember the expression, "You can lead a horse to water but you can't make him . . . . .? Yes, the rest of the statement is the word "drink." It is the same for people, too, isn't it? Unless they have a thirst for God they won't seek Him. Over the years I have talked to lots of pre-Christians, most of whom haven't a clue as to what their real important needs are. They think they need a raise or a better job, a new car, a bigger boat, a better wife, kids who obey, and on it goes. But we know that their primary need is for God's forgiveness.

Why is it that they aren't actively seeking Him and the forgiveness He has provided? I think it's because they aren't aware of how much they need it. Take the assembly to whom Peter spoke on that first Pentecost Sunday. Some seven weeks had elapsed since the crucifixion of Christ. The feast of Pentecost has come and once again the city was filled with Jewish people—many of whom had cried out for Jesus' death earlier. Would they feel the need for God's forgiveness for what they had done?

But something had changed. The early followers of Christ had been in the upper room praying for ten days and then after a sermon by an uneducated fisherman, the people "were cut to the heart and said to Peter and the other apostles, 'Brothers, what shall we do'" (Acts 2:37)? All of a sudden they realized their need. Don't you suppose that the prior ten days of prayer had something to do with that result? Perhaps if we prayed more specifically along these lines others would respond more specifically along the same lines. I think God is still anxious to answer that kind of prayer today. That is why I find myself continually praying that people I know will feel the need for God's forgiveness and be ready when the message comes their way.

Think about the words of Jesus when he said, "No one can come to me unless the Father who sent me draws him" (John 6:44a). Did you notice that He said *no one*? God is directly involved with the process by which cynics become seekers so let's pray that they will be drawn in to Jesus by the Father. I remember so well how I'd visited with a staff member over the course of years about her spiritual needs and her response was, "I guess I'm just too much of a cynic." You can rest assured that I still pray for her to feel the need for God's forgiveness because I know that unless and until she feels that need we can't go on to the next step.

Another Scriptural example comes to mind. Remember when Paul and Silas had been beaten and jailed in Philippi? Their backs were bloody but their hearts were full of joy as they considered themselves fortunate to have been worthy of such suffering for Jesus. I think they were concerned that their accusers would feel the need for God's forgiveness. As they prayed through the long night hours, an earthquake liberated them from their bonds but bound the jailer with fear for his own life. What was his response? "Sirs, what must I do to be saved" (Acts 16:30)? All of a sudden he realized what his greatest need was—to be saved! The first step in praying for the needs of our pre-Christian friends starts here doesn't it?

Pray that they will begin to feel this need deeply, that their hearts will ache from this lack and that other needs will pale into insignificance in comparison. I remember well how I prayed for about three years for a friend along these lines. He is another of my friends made through contacts in the old car hobby. He was thoughtful, pensive, an accountant by training and trade, a detail man with lots of cars and projects who was also willing to help me out with a project now and then.

One day when we were standing at the curb outside his house in the gathering darkness of a warm summer evening he said, "Ron could we get together some time and talk about God?" I replied, "Has God been talking to you about your relationship with Him?" (That's another good opening question in my arsenal.) His lip trembled as he paused, and then said, "That's just the problem. I've been talking to Him but I can't seem to hear Him answer me at all." Finally he began seeking God until it hurt not to have the need met. Now I knew we were making progress. We made an appointment for a few days later and it was great to watch him drink in the necessary truths to meet his spiritual needs. As he prayed to receive God's forgiveness through Christ there was a load that rolled off both of us.

I remember another friend for whom I had been praying. This event happened about 15 years ago. When the opportunity came to talk about spiritual things I asked her if she had ever felt the need for God's forgiveness. She said she had, but was never really sure if God had forgiven her or not. In fact, the whole concept of forgiveness seemed to bring her to tears. I sensed that were was more than the normal pain here so I asked her if she wanted to tell me about it. Then through her sobs she told me that she was soon due to attend the parole hearing for the man who had murdered her sister and left her body in an abandoned rock quarry. God had been connecting her need to forgive others with her need to be forgiven by Him, but she just couldn't understand how either could happen. She didn't know how God's forgiveness really works.

You'll be pleased to know that God soon brought her to the place of releasing it all to Him and receiving His forgiveness for her own sins. In an upcoming chapter I'll share more about how to explain these essential concepts to a seeking heart.

Before we move on to the next way to pray for our pre-Christian friends I must tell you of another encounter I had, this time with an 84-year-old lady who was a resident in an assisted living center where I held weekly Bible studies. She was tall, carried herself with erect posture, always well dressed, obviously well educated and still mentally very sharp. I had visited her off and on for a few years. After many months I still hadn't made much progress with her as far as being able to talk about her personal spiritual needs. She seemed to fend off conversations about spiritual things no matter how I tried to gently direct the conversation.

Finally I just blurted out, "Have you ever felt the need for God's forgiveness?" Her quick reply left me nearly speechless, "Oh, my goodness, no. Not yet!" I immediately wondered what she had planned for the rest of the week! Many months later I attended her funeral and saw a business woman from the city whom I knew to be a Christian, so I approached her and asked how she came to be there. She replied, "Oh, didn't you know? I prayed with her a while back to receive Christ."

Isn't it just great to see how God uses many different people to reach one? It's still just like the Bible says, "I planted the seed, Apollos watered it, but God made it grow" (1 Corinthians 3:6).

I could give many more examples but I certainly must include this one from just this afternoon. A few weeks ago I got a call from "Nancy", a long-time friend whose husband's uncle had recently been placed on hospice. Uncle "Mel" had attended a family function where I had officiated at "Nancy's" 40th wedding anniversary renewal of vows a few years back and he remembered me. He asked "Nancy" to ask me to contact him.

During our first visit he relayed to me much of his life history. During our second visit we went over the obituary information he and his wife "Wendy" had gathered up. On our third visit the conversation went something like this--He started:

"I want you to pray for me."

"Is there anything specifically that you want me to pray about?"

"I want to be baptized."

"Have you come to the place in your spiritual life where you know for sure that when you die you're going to heaven?"

"Yes. Well, I hope so. I guess I'm not very sure."

"Imagine that you're waiting to get into heaven and Jesus asks why He should let you in. What would you say? What reasons would you give Him?"

"Well, I want to. And when you baptize me then I can."

"Before we talk about baptism we need to talk about receiving God's forgiveness. Have you ever felt the need for God's forgiveness?"

". . . . . I'm just trying to worry this out in my head. Yes. I think so."

"Have you ever asked God to forgive you?"

"Yes, with you."

"No, in our previous meetings we've only prayed about physical needs, not spiritual needs. But, by your own admission you understand that unless God forgives you, you won't be going to heaven, is that right?"

"Yes, that's right."

"The Bible says 'If we confess our sins He is faithful and just and will forgive us forgive us our sins'" (I John 1:9). Are you ready to confess your sin and guilt to God?"

"Yes, I am."

After some more conversation I had him say a prayer of confession and repentance, repeating it phrase by phrase after me. Then I knew it was time to move on to the concept of forgiveness being a gift. (See the next section.) He received the gift of a pen from me, thanked me and meant it and was ready to thank God that he was already forgiven. We stopped again to pray an honest prayer of thanks to God.

I'll share more later, but I've seen it so many times that the act of receiving a unique and valuable gift from me is usually enough to trigger the understanding that what God is waiting for is us to quit asking Him to forgive us and for us to simply accept forgiveness as a gift, then thank him and mean it.

Then I told him we could now go on to talk about baptism. After that conversation I had his wife bring out a bowl of water from the kitchen and used some of that to sprinkle baptize him. Then I asked him.

"Did God just meet a spiritual need in your heart?"

"Yes, the guilt is gone. I feel so much better. Thank you. Thank God"

At that moment the doorbell rang, announcing the interruption of our visit by the arrival of the hospice social worker. While I'd been talking and praying with him I'd also been telling Satan to keep away. I was not about to let him have this precious man who was so earnestly seeking God's forgiveness. Now, here's the "fun" part. The whole 35 minutes I was visiting, explaining and praying, this man was on the commode in his front room. Every now then I heard a little bit of tinkling. Definitely a first in my experience!

It was only 41 hours after he prayed that I got a phone call from the nephew letting me know that uncle "Mel" had passed into eternity. It was such a shock because he was so alert, responsive and apparently not in any physical distress. I do truly believe that he knew what he had to do, just needed some help, waited until he got it, found peace with God through forgiveness and couldn't hang on any longer. In fact, as I write this paragraph I'm dressed in a suit because in just a few hours I'll be conducting his memorial service. It will be my great privilege to share his testimony with his family and friends from the American Legion.

A few weeks have passed and I'm back to writing again. I simply must let you know that just two weeks after I conducted his memorial, his wife also prayed through to a place of peace with God. She had her husband's pen on the table and was waiting for me to explain how she could get hers, too. She had only been in the room at the very end of my conversations and prayer time with her husband. What a joy to be there to see her come to faith and freedom as well! Do you see what I mean about initially praying for people to feel the need for God's forgiveness? If they don't, we can't go on in the discussion.

I must also include a few examples here of people for whom I've prayed regularly for many years who have apparently yet to feel the need for God's forgiveness. "Deanna," a staff person in one of my buildings, and I have become friends over the years. She has shared with me of the tragic death of her brother and her struggles with trying to come to peace with God. Some years ago I asked her if it would be okay if she would accept me as a sort of spiritual mentor and she agreed.

When I saw her the next week I gave her a piece of paper on which I had printed these questions: "Have you come to the place in your spiritual life where you know for sure and certain that when you die you will go to heaven and be with Jesus? Suppose you were to die today and Jesus would ask you, 'Why should I let you into heaven?' What reasons would you give Him? Have you ever felt the need for God's forgiveness?"

As she scanned the page I saw her face blanch, then redden as she responded, "I don't think I'm ready for this kind of thing." I assured her that it was okay but I would continue to be available down the road if she ever wanted to talk. Over the intervening years I've kept up with her and even loaned her a book that I thought would be helpful--Phillip Yancey's book, *Disappointment With God*. It took her quite a while to get through it and when she finally returned it to me she was still not ready to talk about her own spiritual needs. She's the one who said that she was just too much of a cynic.

Another example is "Gordon" and "Betty," a couple I have known for 21 years through our mutual interest in the car restoration hobby. After a few years we became friends so I began to ask them about spiritual things. They invited me to their home to talk about it. I remember so well being in their home one evening after I carefully explained the way of salvation and asking them if that made sense and were they ready to receive God's forgiveness as a gift. They both replied, "We're just not ready for that." How disappointed I was and still am. I see them now and then around town. I'm still praying for them and knowing that until and unless they really feel the need for God's forgiveness as their greatest need we can't go any further in the conversation. Can you think of people in your circle of influence for whom you can pray this way? I continue to pray for them and others like them every morning, which brings us to our next focus for intercessory prayer.

GOSPEL, GRACE, GIFT:

These three "G" words are necessary concepts for our pre-Christian friends to understand before they will find peace with God, aren't they? They sure were for me and probably you, too. As I pray for my friends in this area I am constantly drawn to this Biblical truth, "For it is by grace you have been saved, through faith—and this not from yourselves. It is the gift of God, not by works, so that no one can boast" (Ephesians 2:8, 9). Oh, that God would use whatever tools are necessary to bring our friends to a correct understanding of how His grace has provided all they need to be forgiven, to know that the key concept here is gift and they can know it for sure!

So many people, both in and out of the church, have been confused at this point. I'm going to take plenty of time here to explain to you how I explain it to them so they can understand. People may mentally agree with the facts of the gospel: that God the Father can forgive us only because Jesus the Son was punished in our place, that the Father accepted what Jesus did for us on the cross as good as if we'd been able to do it for ourselves and that forgiveness now becomes a *GIFT* planned for by the Father and provided for by the Son. But that doesn't mean they have experienced receiving the gift. Mere mental assent with the facts is not the same as experiencing it personally. It is only the first level of the three kinds of faith. (The others are faith for life's situations and faith for forgiveness that leads to eternal life.) What I've discovered over these decades is that the problem is that most people really *DON'T* understand this most important key.

Let me illustrate. This encounter happened just yesterday. I'd been visiting "Nora" every other week or so for many months in one of my facilities. (For years I've been in at least eight buildings each week as a salaried chaplain. Not so many now that I've retired.) She said so many of the right words. She talked of church involvement, "accepting Jesus," attending Bible studies, etc. but I had always felt that there just might be something missing. For some months her husband had also been in the same facility. He expired there about four months earlier. We had talked about her ongoing grief process. Yesterday she was once again having an especially hard time but on this occasion her struggle was with knowing for sure that God had truly forgiven her past sins.

I began to ask questions. (You will find a list of suggested questions in chapter eight.) "Have you come to the place in your spiritual life where you know for absolute certainty that when you die you will go to heaven and be with Jesus?" Perhaps you recognize that as the first question from the Evangelism Explosion presentation. I still use it a lot but may not always start with it.

She wasn't so sure, so I went on to the next question, "Suppose that you were to die today and you were seated on a park bench at heaven's door waiting your turn to enter and Jesus comes up and asks you, "Why should I let you into heaven?" What would you tell him? What reasons would you give him as to why He should let you into heaven?

"Nora" appeared to be confused as she tried to come up with an answer. "Well, because I love Him," she replied. So I asked her, "What's not to love about Jesus?" "What do you mean?" was her reply. I said, "Can we really take any credit for loving Jesus when that's the easiest thing there is to do? Are there really any reasons not to love Him?"

She began to see there was a problem with her relationship with the Lord but she couldn't really define it. So I pressed on. I was hoping to fill in the blanks, praying that the Holy Spirit would make it plain and all the while asking Jesus to keep Satan at bay.

I asked, "Have you ever felt the need for God's forgiveness?" She had but didn't think He ever had so I knew where the problem lay and pressed on. "Did you know that God forgives us differently than we forgive each other?" KEY QUESTION HERE!

This is where almost all pre-Christians are confused, maybe even you, too, as you read this book. Either way, please pay close attention to what I have to say next. I went on to explain to her first how forgiveness *doesn't* work. What I've learned over the years is that people can't fully understand how God's forgiveness really works until they can see how the ways they try to forgive other people really don't work. I try to get them to see the need to quit using those faulty methods. When they see that they don't work for us then they can see how they can't work for God either. Let me explain.

Here's the first method that doesn't work. Have you ever heard the expression "Forgive and Forget?" Sure you have. Have you ever tried it? Probably. Has it worked? Of course not and here's why. Forgetting is a malfunction of the mind while forgiving is a function of the will—two very different parts of our psyche. We can't choose to forget, can we? Since we can't, then we also can't take credit for it. "Ah, yes, now I've successfully forgotten what so-and-so did to me last Wednesday at around 4:52 as we were getting ready to leave work." See there, you just remembered it.

That's why the old "Forgive and Forget" method never has worked. If it doesn't work for us why do we expect God to use it on our behalf? Too many times people just hope that God loses track of our sins because He doesn't really pay all that much attention. Does God have a faulty memory or does He make wise choices instead? I think it's the latter. Some of you may be getting ready to straighten me out here because the Bible says God doesn't remember our sins, but if you'll pay close attention you'll find that He doesn't remember--or hold--them *against us* any more. God has chosen not to hold us accountable because he has chosen to punish Christ for our guilt. That choice of His reveals a much different approach than just hoping that God's memory will fail him at the crucial moment for us when we face heaven's gate.

While you're thinking on that, let's move on to another method of forgiving that doesn't work. Let's pretend that someone purposefully made your job harder at work and you found out about it. Now the culprit just found out that you've discovered the truth. What does he do?

Does he own up to his misbehavior or try the old method of using the double pronged approach of ignoring his guilt and being extra nice to you. He may even volunteer to give you his "Employee of the Month" parking space for the remainder of the month because you have a cold and he doesn't want you to have to walk any farther in the rain than necessary. Next, he volunteers to get treats for the crew even though it's your turn and everyone knows it. What's he doing? He's trying to balance out bad behavior with good behavior. But that actually makes it harder for you to forgive him, doesn't it? You just want him to come clean, admit his guilt, say he's sorry and mean it so your relationship can start over.

Don't we all have that same imaginary balance scale in the back of our head? Don't we tend to use it on God, thinking that a change in our behavior will make it easier for Him to forgive us? As Christians we don't anymore, but let me tell you that pre-Christians do. I could give you a great number of examples of this confusion in the minds of so many pre-Christians I have talked with.

Over and over I see people trying to use this method of "forgiveness." It takes a while for them to see its faults but with some help they eventually do. I have to explain that to them and get them to abandon their insistence on using this failed method with God. After all, if we can see right through it as a failed attempt in our efforts to forgive each other, certainly God can see through it, too. Because He isn't impressed a bit when we try it out on him we simply must abandon this failed system and no longer try it on him.

The third and most commonly used but failed method of forgiveness can best be illustrated this way. Pretend that you're a five-year-old in a big family, waiting to get a plateful of Thanksgiving dinner from your mom. She fills a plate for you and then directs you to a place across the room to sit with your cousins on the hearth or stairway. On the way there you trip over Grandpa's cane and "baptize" his lap with turkey, dressing, potatoes and gravy.

As you burst into tears, looking for Mom, she assures you that if you just go talk to Grampa and tell him you're sorry he'll forgive you. You do and Grampa pats you on the head, takes your face in his tender hands and says, "Now punkin,' don't you worry; I know you didn't mean to spill. We'll clean up the mess; you just try harder next time, okay? I forgive you." Sort of reminds you of how Santa Claus might do it, doesn't it?

Now I ask you, did Grampa forgive you? While you might think so, and you might know that he had the best of intentions, he did *not* forgive you. I know you're shocked and ready to come to the defense of your Grandpa's character but let me prove it to you with another illustration that may seem over the top, so to speak, but bear with me. I think that you will see that it is sometimes necessary to stretch the point to make the point.

Just imagine that it's ten years later. Now you're 15 and you and a cousin find a pistol in Uncle Larry's desk, bring it out to the dining room and shoot Aunt Mae through the heart! Will Grandpa just say the same thing this time? "Now punkin,' don't worry, I know you didn't mean to. We'll clean up the mess; you just try harder next time, okay? I forgive you." Not at all! Why? Because in the first example Grandpa didn't really forgive, he was just pretending it didn't matter. The second time it did matter and this method of "forgiving" just won't work unless it doesn't matter, will it? (What do we do when it really matters?)

But isn't this the most common and socially acceptable way we "forgive" each other? We don't really forgive we just pretend it doesn't matter, don't we? That's alright, though. That's how we get along socially.

Then why can't God use this method to forgive us? Because our sins caused the horrible death of His Son right in the living room of world history! Our sins simply can't be overlooked any more than what you and your cousin did in the illustration above can be ignored. Pretending is doesn't matter will never be equal to genuine forgiveness.

There is a proverb which says, "It is to a man's glory to overlook an offense" (Proverbs 19:11). That's true, we do look better when we overlook the offensive ways of those around us, but God can't do that because what we did has eternal consequences and therefore *does* matter. It can't simply be overlooked. No amount of pretending it doesn't matter can diminish its consequence.

Let's go another step deeper here. I know we're in a section regarding how to pray effectively for pre-Christians, but this information is critically important for you to understand so you can in turn help them to understand. People often mistakenly think that God forgives us the way we try to forgive each other. He doesn't. I've listed all three of the ways we try to forgive each other. None of them really works between ourselves so why do we insist that God must use any of these? He can't; He won't and it's unreasonable to expect Him to.

Now that I've destroyed your fondly held suppositions about forgiveness, let me explain what forgiveness really is and how it *does* work. Briefly stated, *forgiveness is accepting payment from someone other than the one who is indebted to you as good as if that person had paid it himself.* At least that's where it starts.

Let me use another example to help make it clear. Let's pretend that I borrow ten thousand dollars from you and agree to pay it back at the rate of five hundred dollars each month. Ten months later I'm half way through paying my debt to you when I quit paying. Now you have an opportunity to forgive me of five thousand dollars. Notice that I made the dollar amount large enough so that you couldn't just use the pretending-it-doesn't-matter method of forgiveness. If I had only borrowed ten dollars and failed to repay half of that you could easily pretend it didn't matter because it really didn't. Overlooking a missing five dollar bill is not too difficult. However missing five thousand dollars really does matter; at least it would to me.

Now what is it going to take for you to forgive me? Well five thousand dollars for starters, isn't it? There are only three sources for the money that I can think of, short of you finding it on the pavement between cars in the Wal-Mart parking lot. Here they are: The money may come from me, a friend, or from yourself.

Now here's where it gets difficult for you to forgive. Since I don't have it to repay you, that uses up the first of the three sources for the money. Let's move on to the second. If I had a friend who came to you and offered the money to you to pay my debt would you accept it? Of course you would accept the money, but would you accept it as good as if I'd paid it to you myself on time? Not very likely. Now let's make it even harder by moving on to the third and final source of the repayment. Would you be able to take it from your vacation fund and put it in to the bad-debts-from-the-chaplain fund and still be able to accept it as good as if I'd paid it to you myself on time? Extremely unlikely! But that is the only way true forgiveness works. That is how God's forgiveness works.

"How does it work," you ask? "How can I truly forgive someone and also truly know that I've successfully done it?" If you were able to accept payment from any source but me you would have to go through a series of four steps. Doing so would confirm to you that you really had forgiven me. Let me explain.

First, you wouldn't talk to me about the debt since you'd accepted payment already from another source. That's hard, isn't it? Second you wouldn't talk to others about my dereliction of duty. That's even harder. What would you say if someone would come to you to ask your advice about whether they should loan me money? Be careful now. You accepted payment in full as good as if I'd done it myself didn't you?

Okay, let's move on to the third level of difficulty. You wouldn't talk to yourself about it. No more punching the pillow at night, no debt regrets or loan remorse. After all, my debt was paid and you accepted payment as good as if I'd paid it myself on time, didn't you? There is one more level of difficulty to go, the fourth. When (or if) we really forgive someone this way, (which, by the way, is the only true kind of forgiveness) we will also refuse to let the past experience change our current or future relationship.

Allow me to give a small example from my own experience. About 30 years ago we were able to have a house built when we were pastoring in Spokane, WA. In it we had a fan with a three-speed switch and a three-speed motor to evacuate the hot summer air from the house. One very hot, summer day the next year the switch went bad--no moving air--resulting in a hot house and a cranky family.

One of our friends at the Christian school where I was teaching owned a hardware store not far from our house. In fact his daughter played Varsity girls basketball and our son Brian played JV boys basketball. We two dads frequently sat together on the bleachers because her game preceded Brian's. I called him at the store with my problem. He said to come on down and he'd fix me up.

Well, he only had a two-speed switch. Now I was thinking, "Did we ever use the medium speed? Not really; it was pretty much either high or low." I agreed to the two-speed switch but there weren't as many wires on the new switch as on the old one and the colors weren't the same either. I had made a careful chart of how ours was wired in before I left the house. He looked at it and said there wouldn't be a problem. He drew up a new chart for me and sent me on my way. I wired it in exactly like he had said, then called him back just to be sure. I grew up pulling wires for my dad on the farm so this wasn't a scary task at all.

I put the "juice" to it and guess what? No, I wasn't that lucky. You just thought that it didn't work at all. Wrong! It absolutely fried the motor. Because we now we had a house rapidly filling up with the acrid smell of burning motor windings I had the opportunity to forgive him not only for a three dollar switch but a thirty dollar motor! And this was back when thirty dollars was worth quite a bit more than it is now.

I was so cranked out with him that I would not even buy a shovel at his store. Come on, now. How many moving parts are there in a shovel to go wrong? That just shows how much I needed to work my way through the steps of genuine forgiveness.

Here's how I knew I'd truly forgiven him of this problem that was way too small to be major but just a bit too big to be minor, especially with the funds we had available at the time. I worked myself through the four steps I mentioned above. I refused to talk to him about it, to others about it, to myself about or let it hinder our relationship.

The way I knew I'd finally gotten through step four was a year later when I bought paint from his store for the new garage we built. It did feel good to know in my own heart that I'd forgiven him. Was that a small thing? Sure, but it does illustrate the point. At least I hope it does. The principle and the steps are the same no matter how minor or major the offense.

Now some of you are beginning to wonder how I could have gotten so far afield in the discussion. We were supposed to be talking about praying that our pre-Christian friends would understand that the gospel is the message of the gift of God's grace in the form of forgiveness. I had to help you to understand first of all how forgiveness doesn't work, and then how it does work in order for you to plainly see how I explain to someone that forgiveness must always be a *gift*.

Remember, *forgiveness is accepting payment from someone other than the one who is indebted to you as good as if that person had paid it himself*. What I have just explained to you so far is very close to how I explain it to a seeker.

Here is where I pull out my secret weapon. Most of the time as I've been explaining these important truths to someone, I've also been writing, outlining and charting this information with one of my *magic telescoping pens*. That's why I prefer to be sitting at a table where I can sit next to someone so they can watch as I outline these points on paper. When the pens are collapsed, the point disappears to keep your pocket clean and when it is extended the point reappears. They are attractive not only because of their usefulness but also because of their rarity. They are also beautifully designed and are not inexpensive. I always carry at least one in my pocket. Every morning as I start my day I take one off the top of my dresser and put it in my pants pocket with a prayer that God will bring someone along who wants to know the truth about genuine forgiveness.

After I have shown them the pen I will say something like this to them: "About 20 minutes ago I gave you this pen. It really is quite unique. When it telescopes in it shortens down to about half its length and the point disappears so your pocket and hands stay clean. Pull it out to full length again and the point reappears. Isn't it a great pen? Earlier I used an illustration, a story of my borrowing ten thousand dollars from you. That was just pretend, wasn't it? Well now, this is for real. This is your pen. I bought it myself and I gave it to you just a bit ago but you didn't know it then, did you? Well, now you know. So let me ask you a very simple question: 'Is this your pen?'"

Usually the person will pause, look at me questioningly, think a bit and then reply, "No." That's when I usually ask them, "Why not? You aren't calling me a liar are you?" I remind them this is *not* just an illustration; this is the truth. After a bit more conversation they usually agree, however grudgingly. While I am still holding the pen in my hand, I ask them, "Why is it that I don't quite believe you yet? When you receive a gift from someone what do you usually do?"

Soon they'll catch on that they need to take it from my hand. If not, I'll say, "So, I'm waiting" and just smile. Somewhere in the process it usually begins to dawn on them that this unique and beautiful new pen really is theirs and they will thank me for it. But I'm not finished. I've learned that there are still some new vistas that need to be opened up in their spirit.

Because this person usually has a ways to go yet, I get out one of my business cards and suggest that they write me a thank you note with their new pen. After they do and give it to me I point out to them that this isn't just a thank you note; it's really a receipt. After all it has all the things necessary for something to be a receipt: it's written out, dated, itemized and signed. As they are holding the pen and I'm holding the receipt I may say to them, "You know, the first time you verbally thanked me I think you may have just been giving me a socially polite response. Now I want you to look me in the eyes, thank me for the pen and really mean it this time."

It is right here that many times they will catch on that this is how God wants us to accept forgiveness from Him--as a gift. The reason it's not ours is because we've never received it and sincerely thanked Him for it. I cannot begin to tell you how many times I've seen the miracle of faith take place at this important juncture. It is here that I see so many people receive God's forgiveness and know it for the first time in their lives.

Let me illustrate. Many years ago I was in the home of an acquaintance at the invitation of a family member to answer her questions about just this subject. Before I went to talk with her I asked my wife and others to pray that she would receive the spiritual clarity to grasp the concept that forgiveness is a gift of God's grace.

I will always remember what happened as I was explaining to her that when Jesus was punished for our sins He was paying our spiritual debts and the miracle of it all is that God the Father accepted that payment as good as if she had been able to make it herself. All she had to do was the same thing—accept the payment as good as if she'd paid it and then accept God's forgiveness as a gift already given, but just not accepted yet.

As I was holding out the pen in my hand waiting for her to receive it as a gift, all of a sudden her whole face changed. In just a few seconds she grew somber, her eyes teared up, and then her whole face beamed with joy. She came around the dining room table to give me a warm hug. I said, "You just figured it out didn't you?" Through her tears of joy she readily agreed. I knew then that God had just met her spiritual need—but we prayed anyway to thank Him that He already had! See how that works?

HOLY SPIRIT TO REMOVE HINDRANCES:

Here are the "H" words as we now continue in our alphabetical prayer guide. Have you ever spent much time thinking of the hindrances to faith that there may be in your friends' minds and lives? I'm convinced that many times God is waiting for His people to pray that the Holy Spirit would remove them. Recall with me the promise Jesus gave His disciples, "But when he, the Spirit of truth, comes, he will guide you into all truth. He will not speak on his own; he will speak only what he hears, and he will tell you what is yet to come" (John 16:13).

Okay, so let's pray that the Holy Spirit would come that way in specific people's lives, bearing in mind these Bible truths: "Those who live according to the sinful nature have their minds set on what that nature desires; but those who live in accordance with the Spirit have their minds set on what the Spirit desires because those who are led by the Spirit of God are the sons of God" (Romans 8:5, 14). As I pray, I ask the Holy Sprit to remove the hindrances of evil friends, bad memories and any grudges they may hold against other people, especially Christians. As you pray, you may begin to become aware of some more particular ways to focus your prayer energy for a specific individual's needs, I'm sure.

Here is another example from the Bible. Do you recall the time the prophet Elisha was in Dothan and enemy soldiers surrounded the city under cover of darkness? While his servant was in a panic, Elisha asked the Lord to open the servant's eyes to see the whole situation. The servant was blinded to the Lord's presence by his focus on trying to count how many soldiers surrounded them. That was his hindrance. Don't we all do that from time to time? We get so focused on all the reasons why God can't help that we forget to look for his presence. Check out the Bible to see how that need was met. "And Elisha prayed, 'O Lord, open his eyes so he may see.' Then the Lord opened the servant's eyes, and he looked and saw the hills full of horses and chariots of fire all around Elisha" (2 Kings 6:17).

Let me tell you about "Ted," a hospice patient at one of my buildings. He would be an example of this need for the Holy Spirit to remove the spiritual hindrances to his coming to faith. There were obvious signs that his health was gradually failing. He was losing weight; he was looking grayer every week and he was on a pain pump that he used as a worry rock most of the time. (You do know, of course, that those machines are calibrated in such a way as to prevent the patient from overdosing himself.)

When I first met him I noticed a Buddha statue on the table by the window. Starting with my usual opening round of get acquainted questions he soon interrupted me by demanding, "How long will this inquisition last?" Yes, he was a bit hostile, so I tried to ease his fears on that initial visit. I kept coming back every week, though. My prayer for him started with asking God to help him come to the place where he would feel the need for forgiveness as his greatest need, but quickly I moved on to praying that the Holy Spirit would remove the hindrances to his seeing that "the one who is in you is greater than the one who is in the world" (1 John 4:4). I felt that he needed to know from God Himself that Buddha couldn't hold a candle to Jesus!

I kept praying to the Lord and talking with Ted. Some many weeks later he was ready with his questions about end of life issues. One day without warning he blurted out, "Will I go to Heaven? What will it be like? Will I have a body? What will that be like?" It was like scales had come off his eyes; he was ready to hear the truth and receive forgiveness as a gift. I took him through the conversation about forgiveness and gifts as I recorded it earlier in this book and soon Ted found peace with God. We had many good visits after that until he passed away a few months later.

Another example of a person needing the Holy Spirit to remove spiritual hindrances in her life was "Evelyn." Her story and situation, however, are quite the opposite of "Ted's." She was active in an evangelical, Bible-believing church her whole adult life. Over those years she had led many women's Bible studies and had taught children in Vacation Bible School. Finally she had to give up her house and come to live in an assisted living facility where I regularly held Bible studies and visited with the residents.

I had known her for years through the church connection with my grandparents but I felt that there were hindrances to her coming to Christ that she had been experiencing all those years. They ended up being the hindrances of faithful Christian service. I can almost hear some of you asking, "How can that be a hindrance?" Here is how:

she had let faithfulness become a substitute for faith. In her mind faithfulness to the work of the church had made a personal surrender to Christ unnecessary. I'm convinced that she's not alone. I believe there are lots of folks in our churches just like her who have depended on faithful activity to substitute for realizing that they need God's forgiveness in order for them to ever see heaven.

As I worked through the explanations of how forgiveness doesn't work, then how it works, and finally how it's always a gift, I held out one of those "magic pens," waiting for her to reach out and accept it as a gift. I could see the changes in her heart becoming apparent on her face as she understood for the first time what she had been missing all those years. It was just a few short weeks later that I was able to tell her story during the memorial service held in her own church. As I was speaking, I was also praying that God's Spirit would remove the hindrances in the lives of those who attended.

IGNORE IDOLS:

As you look as this prayer topic you're probably thinking that no one worships idols around here any more. So how would you define an idol? Most Christians will probably say that an idol is defined as anything that comes between a person and God. While that may be true, I think that the definition needs to be both refined and broadened in order to get at the rest of the truth—in order to see the *whole* truth. In order to do that we need to think about how we order our priorities.

In your own mind put everything you have, are and do in a list with the most important at the top. To make the process easy let's say there are only 15 such items. (In reality the list would probably be much longer.) It is easy for us to say that God is at the top, but what does that look like on any given day? How do we measure that? Do we measure it by how much time we spend in daily Bible reading and private worship? In church attendance? In involvement in outreach activities? In helping the needy? The answers to those questions is probably "Yes," but much more thought needs to be given to this important subject. We do that by spending time with God listening to Him and tweaking the list, don't we?

Now look at your list of 15. Suppose God has got you all sorted out so that they are all in perfect order from first to fifteenth according to value from *HIS* perspective. Now suppose that over time you let number eight move down a few places, or you let number twelve move up a few places. What does that do to all those in between? It moves them, too, doesn't it?

Here is the principle we observe: <u>whenever we</u> <u>elevate anything to a higher place of importance than it really has from God's perspective</u> we inadvertently skew our whole value system. It's the old law of unintended consequences, isn't it? The value of some things ends up inflated, while others are deflated.

Here is the second observable principle: <u>God classes an idol as anything to which we give more value than He does—even a little bit.</u>

For example, putting your kids to bed at night and membership in a church ministry team are both admirable; neither one is between us and God. But are they equal in value from God's perspective? What if they aren't in the right order from God's point of view? Won't that upset the rest of life's commitments? Even a little bit? What do you think? All I'm saying as I think "out loud on paper" is that maybe we need to do some more work in this area ourselves as Christians.

Since it is by our values that we make decisions, how can our pre-Christian friends make appropriate spiritual decisions unless and until they come to the place where they are willing to realign the things they formerly held in a place of honor, putting them only in the order that God would. This will require both prayerful thought and careful action.

As an example, observe the actions of those early Ephesian Christians. "Many of those who believed now came and openly confessed their evil deeds. A number who had practiced sorcery brought their scrolls together and burned them publicly. When they calculated the value of the scrolls, the total came to fifty thousand drachmas" (Acts 19:18, 19). A drachma was a coin worth about a day's wage. In today's currency and wages of about ten dollars an hour for ten hours, or one hundred dollars a day, that would be five million dollars worth! Do you think that kind of behavioral change came about without focused prayer? These people were willing to ignore the idols that the Holy Spirit had revealed in their lives.

Can you see that this prayer focus is so closely linked to the previous one? Having the Holy Spirit remove the spiritual hindrances in their lives was only one step; the next step was their responsibility--to ignore the idols He revealed. Can you see how "Ted" went through both steps, and in that order? That is the way I pray for folks who have heard the message but don't yet feel the need for God's forgiveness. It all goes together in a linked chain.

GOD'S JUDGMENT WILL BE JUST:

Here are our "J" words—judgment and just. Have you noticed that many people these days express the opinion that no one has the right to judge them in any respect? In fact to do so is a sin in itself, according to them. Their concept of God is One who will just pretend that the sins they have committed don't really matter after all. They're hoping that He will just pat them on the head and say, "That's okay, I know you didn't mean it. I'll clean up the mess. You just try harder next time and I'll forgive you." Of course that isn't even an accurate picture of how a well run kindergarten operates, much less the universe. But we've already covered that subject of how forgiveness doesn't work earlier in this book, haven't we?

Jesus Himself spoke of the eternal nature of God's judgment when he said, "Depart from me, you who are cursed, into the eternal fire, prepared for the devil and his angels" (Matthew 25:41). We must pray that the pre-Christians in our sphere of influence will be brought to the realization that after death we will "meet our Maker" as the Bible says, "Just as man is destined to die once, and after that to face judgment. . ." (Hebrews 9:27). Yes, there will be judgment for sin—just as sure as death itself. When pre-Christians understand that truth, they are much more likely to become seekers, aren't they? That's why I pray that way.

This spiritually unsettling truth will need to be spiritually communicated and for that we need specific prayer for the Spirit's intervention. He is the one who can best deliver this sobering truth. Personally, I don't work at making that truth clear because I know that the Holy Spirit can and will do it much more effectively than I ever could. A person can reject my words as just an expression of my opinion, but when the Holy Spirit brings that truth home they can't ignore it.

The message delivery may very well come in the form of circumstances, not just through changed thought patterns. For instance, do you remember the response of the observers to the deaths of Ananias and his wife Saphira, "Great fear seized the whole church and all who heard about these events" (Acts 5:10-11)?

It is true that we must be "ready to give an answer," as the Scripture says, and that surely does apply to this subject of eternal punishment in a hell that was never intended for people, only for the devil and his angels. But it is also true that here more than in any other place we need to let the Holy Spirit change hearts. So I pray that the Holy Spirit will break through in this area, too. If I am specifically asked about this subject I will answer with the words of Jesus. Otherwise I will let the Holy Spirit bring the truth home.

Even the best loved, most memorized verse in the Bible brings this truth out: "For God so loved the world that He gave His one and only Son, that whoever believes in him shall not *perish* but have eternal life" (John 3:16). It is only as people begin to realize that there will be an eternal accounting for their sins that they will earnestly seek God and His forgiveness. That's why one of the questions I frequently use with seekers is, "Have you sinned enough to keep you out of heaven?" See chapter eight for a fuller treatment of suggested questions to use in guiding the conversation with a seeker.

Well there's "F" through "J." Here's an example of how you might pray for your pre-Christian friends.

"Heavenly Father, as I think about N____, I ask that you will intervene in his life so that he will Feel the need for your Forgiveness deeper than he ever has before--deep enough to do something about it. I pray that he would see that Forgiveness is the most important need that he has; that all those other so-called needs are just temporary inconveniences at their worst. I ask that he would also begin to understand that your Grace has provided this forgiveness as a Gift. That he wouldn't get trapped into thinking that if he just changes his behavior it will somehow make it easier for you to forgive him when you've provided it already as a Gift. Oh, Holy Spirit, won't you follow him around and be at work in him, removing the various Hindrances in his life—the ones he is aware of and the ones only You can perceive at this point. Perhaps he's had some bad history with a Christian. God, don't let him hold that against you and your precious Son. As the Spirit works in his life I pray that N_____ will soon be able to willingly Ignore the Idols in his life. I ask that he will be able to differentiate true value from temporary utility through the direct teaching of your Sprit. And finally, I ask that you would graciously reveal to him that your Judgment is Just, sure, true and final. I pray that he will be thinking about his own mortality and be ready to come to you, in the name of our Lord, Jesus Christ. Amen.

I realize that the way I've structured this chapter may have seemed a bit disjointed but I wanted to deal with these three things simultaneously: an outline of how to pray for our pre-Christian friends, an outline of how I explain the necessary truths of the gospel to seekers and examples of many people who have actually experienced this.

6

PRAYING FOR THE WORLD: A DISCIPLESHIP TOOL

Now let's broaden our prayer horizons to the next level and use this same pattern to focus on ways Christians both new and more mature can pray for the spiritual needs of the world at large. Remember that my focus all along has been three-fold: to explain how I help people understand how God's forgiveness really works, to give examples of how that has worked out for them and to give a practical outline of how to pray for each other as Christians as well as how to pray for pre-Christians.

Let me tie this in with the ministry of personal evangelism. We surely can't just pray with seekers as they accept God's gift of forgiveness and then leave them alone. We do new Christians a great disservice if we don't begin to disciple them along in the faith. There are a great many sources of printed materials to be used in discipleship and follow up with new Christians. I won't try to list all of them or endorse any of them in this volume. But I will urge you to use these following specific targets in prayer to help bring new believers to a deeper level of commitment to the King and a deeper understanding of their new role in the Kingdom.

Teaching Christians how to pray is as essential now as it was when Jesus responded to his disciples' request, "Lord, teach us to pray" (Luke

11:1). Even though they were in the physical presence of the Messiah, they realized their need to go up a notch to the next level of intimacy with the heavenly Father. I think that new Christians today also quickly become aware of their need to be able to communicate with the Lord on a deeper level than when they were first introduced to Him. So let's help them achieve that goal. Let's teach them to pray for the spiritual needs of as much of the world as they can conceive.

If we stopped at praying just for ourselves as fellow Christians and for those individuals to whom we are currently ministering, wouldn't we be leaving out what else is on God's heart? As we look at these final five ways to pray, I ask you to see them as part of our Great Commission responsibility as well as an opportunity to help new Christians grow in maturity. I will once again be using the alphabet as an outline for prayer topics. So let's work our way from "K" through "O".

YOUR KINGDOM COME:

Jesus taught his followers that the Kingdom of God was both present and future; it is also here on earth and in heaven. But the real key to the realm of the present Kingdom is that it exists wherever the King is allowed to rule. That's why as we pray for our world, one of the most important things we can pray for is that Christ will return and set up His Kingdom in person It was promised to the disciples at Jesus' ascension when the angels said, "This same Jesus, who has been taken from you into heaven, will come back in the same way you have seen him go into heaven" (Acts 1:11).

Does that mean that because it's sure to happen we don't need to pray for it? Hardly. Since Jesus instructed his followers then to earnestly pray for the coming of the Kingdom, we are still under that same mandate, aren't we? In fact, that's the final heartbeat of the Bible as revealed in the last chapter of the Biblical record: "The Spirit and the bride say, 'Come!' And let him who hears say, 'Come'" (Revelation 22:17)!

Jesus also told many parables which expressed His perspective on the coming Kingdom and our relationship to it. Matthew chapter thirteen has quite an extensive list. Jesus also summarized our stake in it when He told his followers "Because you have been trustworthy in a very small matter, take charge of ten cities" (Luke 19:17). Being assigned responsibility to care for one of the Lord's cities does sound like Kingdom business, doesn't it?

Some have accused Christians of being so heavenly minded that they are of no earthly use. I'm afraid that too many contemporary Christians may be just the opposite—so earthly minded that they are of no heavenly use! Wouldn't you agree with me that we must rekindle our sense of Kingdom awareness, Kingdom perspective and Kingdom obligations through a concerted, specific prayer focus? I firmly believe that it pleases both the Son and the Father when we do.

Let me give a brief word of caution before I go on, however. I'm afraid that there may be many Christians in this current generation who are pining away for the return of Christ to set up His earthly kingdom simply because they don't want to labor in the harvest fields anymore. I think you will agree with me again that fatigue and laziness are inappropriate motives for praying that Jesus would return to set up His kingdom quickly. Don't you think that we should rather be more concerned that Jesus receives the honor due to Him than we receive the rest we think we are owed? Again, just a thought.

<u>LABORERS:</u>

Now here's another prayer request directly from Jesus: "After this the Lord appointed seventy-two others and sent them two by two ahead of him to every town and place where he was about to go. He told them, 'The harvest is plentiful, but the workers are few. Ask the Lord of the harvest, therefore, to send out workers into his harvest field'" (Luke 10:1-2). Surely if prayer for laborers was needed then, it's needed now!

Have you noticed that our church bulletins may often contain pleas for additional workers to help staff our church programs but may have never started the process with focused, earnest prayer? We go to seminars on how to recruit, train and keep our workers and that may be all well and good. But how much more importance did Jesus give to asking the Heavenly Father to raise them up. Perhaps we've grown too used to usurping the work of the Spirit in this regard. Do you remember that even Jesus, in preparation for calling out his initial twelve disciples, spent a whole night in prayer to the Father? When we do pray for laborers are we really praying for God to raise up helpers for *us* so we don't have to work so hard or for *Him* for His glory?

Another aspect of praying for laborers might go beyond merely praying for new recruits, to praying for the ones we already have so that they will be ready to be fruitful workers in the harvest. Perhaps we haven't seen the answer to our prayers for new laborers because we haven't properly or adequately discipled the ones we do have. Perhaps.

I fear that sometimes another indication of the shallowness of our prayers in this area is that we may simply have allowed pondering to substitute for praying. I'm not meaning to be harsh, but think about it with me, are we really praying for the Father to meet this Kingdom need or are we just pondering on the need itself? Either way we must not neglect this important area of prayer.

MISSIONARY EFFORTS:

As we have our prayer horizons expanded we begin now to pray for missionaries we know who are stationed around the world. Let me suggest that we might also profitably go beyond that and pray for missionaries we *don't* know. Yes, try it.

How about praying for the differing emphases of ministry, too: Bible correspondence courses with people to write them and administer them; Bible translation work that includes those who reduce a spoken language to writing, gain understanding of it, translate the Bible into it, edit their work, publish it and distribute it; media ministries that would surely include radio, television and video production and presentation, (the Jesus Video would be an example); medical ministries of many sorts including nurses, doctors, dentists, opticians, hospitals, dispensaries, sanitariums, leprosariums and on it goes; evangelism ministries that might target children, youth, international students, working adults, retired or institutionalized adults, prison ministries, sports ministries, and on it goes.

You get the idea. Let your imagination get going to pray for these and many other types of outreach and discipleship ministries. Isn't that much better than just saying, "Bless the missionaries with whatever they need to do whatever it is they do." Honestly, I've actually heard prayers just like that! You may already be thinking, "This is going to take more time than I've been giving to prayer!" I remember that discovery, too. Maybe it's time for more Christians to invest more time in Kingdom work through intercessory prayer.

NATIONS OF THE WORLD:

The psalmist said, "Ask of me, and I will make the nations your inheritance, the ends of the earth your possession" (Psalm 2:8). While I understand that this is primarily a Messianic prophecy, I believe that it can also refer to the Church's interest in reaching the entire world for Christ. For instance, Paul made the case for it this way: "I urge, then, first of all, that requests, prayers, intercessions and thanksgiving be made for everyone—for kings and all those in authority, that we may live peaceful and quiet lives in all godliness and holiness. This is good, and pleases God our Savior, who wants all men to be saved and to come to a knowledge of the truth" (1 Timothy 2:1-4).

Will you accept the challenge to begin to read the newspaper and watch the news with new eyes for intercession? When you do, every item will become a prayer request—especially the international news stories. Here's another helpful suggestion: in your prayer book you probably have the seven days of the week listed with items of intercession for each day. Since there are seven continents, why not list one continent for special prayer each day of the week. (Yes, even Antarctica. After all, people are living there six months at a time who are isolated from the world. They also have plenty of time on their hands to ponder their spiritual needs.)

Then, as you pray, try to remember what's been happening in the places that have been in the news. Try to recall as many countries in the "continent of the day" as you can and pray for them by name. Consult a map to learn more. You still may not be able to use that added knowledge to get on a television quiz show, but you'll begin to sense the heart of Jesus when he looked out over the city of Jerusalem and said, "O, Jerusalem, Jerusalem., how often I have longed to gather your children together as a hen gathers her chicks under her wings, but you were not willing" (Matthew 23:37). As we pray, it might also prove beneficial for us to remember Peter's personal knowledge of God's love when he said, "He is patient with you, not wanting anyone to perish, but everyone to come to repentance" (2 Peter 3:9).

Here are a number of Scripture passages that reveal God's interest in the nations of the world. "And this gospel of the kingdom will be preached in the whole world as a testimony to all nations, and then the end will come" (Matthew 24:14). Notice that *all* are included in God's invitation. Can we see that God will do everything possible to make sure that all get the message? As we pray along these lines I am confident that we will discover God's heart finding a larger home in our hearts.

Or how about Jesus' indictment against the religious leaders of his day when he said, "Is it not written: 'My house will be called a house of prayer for all nations'? But you have made it a 'den of robbers.'" (Mark 11:17). Friends, how can *all* nations be included in God's house and his family, unless we include them in our intercessory prayer life?

Many years ago when this began to become a part of my prayer life, I noticed a radical change in how I viewed the world and all its places and peoples. I began to become more of a *world Christian*. God increasingly revealed to me how He felt about the people of the world and how He hurts over them until they come into His Kingdom. I'm sure He will do that for you, too. Look for that change as you enter in to this kind of praying. Surely you can recall with me that after the fall of the Soviet Union's hold on its satellite countries we only then began to learn of the years of concerted, specific prayer from so many sources that had been offered for the spiritual needs of those peoples and countries by name. See there, this kind of prayer *does* work.

What is next? Where else might God want us to break out in a new kind of prayer? That brings us to our final topic.

OPEN DOORS OF OPPORTUNITIES:

We can't think of praying doors open without noticing at least some of the instances where that happened in Scripture. Take a look at these examples:

"But I will stay on at Ephesus until Pentecost, because a great door for effective work has opened to me, and there are many who oppose me" 1 Corinthians 16:8-9). "Now when I went to Troas to preach the gospel of Christ and found that the Lord had opened a door for me. . . ." (2 Corinthians 2:12). In other cases Paul asked his friends to pray that doors would be opened for him. "And pray for us, too, that God may open a door for our message, so that we may proclaim the mystery of Christ" (Colossians 4:3). It worked for him, didn't it? Surely we, too, must engage in this same kind of praying, following Biblical examples. Can you think of closed doors that the Lord would want you to pray open? Sure you can. Then let's do it.

But our focus must not be just on opening political doors, but also on praying open personal spiritual doors, as well. Notice the result of that kind of praying in these two Bible examples: "One of those listening was a woman named Lydia, a dealer in purple cloth from the city of Thyatira, who was a worshiper of God. The Lord opened her heart to respond to Paul's message" (Acts 16:14). And "Here I am! I stand at the door and knock. If anyone hears my voice and opens the door, I will come in and eat with him, and he with me" (Revelation 3:20).

In the first, Paul noticed that the Lord had already opened Lydia's heart and in the second, the Lord Himself is seen standing at closed doors waiting for them to open so He can enter to fulfill every heart's deepest needs. Now that we have seen both kinds of doors, we can pray for both kinds of needs. What an incentive to pray!

In conclusion, here is how a prayer for the world might look as we work our way through the prayer topics designated by the letters "K" through "O."

"Lord of heaven, I ask that just as surely as you are the King there, that you would be the only King here--King of every part of my life today, especially King of my decision-making processes and problem-solving opportunities. May your literal earthly Kingdom soon be ushered in with the arrival of King Jesus to take up the throne of authority that is rightfully His.

For that to happen I ask that you would supernaturally raise up Laborers for the task. Forgive me, Father, for giving in to the temptation to rely on my skills as a recruiter of Laborers when that is rightfully the place of your Spirit. Would You lay your hand on the ones you want, not the ones I think I need. Remind me of what you taught Samuel when you gave him the task of anointing a new king for Israel after Saul's rebellion, 'Man looks on the outward appearance, but the Lord looks at the heart' (1 Samuel 16:7).

Father, I pray for those you've chosen and are currently Ministering around the world right now—those I know and those I don't know. May your protection surround their efforts and may those efforts be crowned with success as they teach, heal, minister, broadcast, travel and much more. (Here's where you can get more specific.)

Lord of the nations, come and brood over these Nations until they hear your voice. I pray for North America, from the sparsely populated Northwest Territories with its Inuit and Eskimo inhabitants through the cities of Canada on down through my beloved United States—all 50 of them—who are in such desperate spiritual need. Bless our President, his cabinet and their staffs with the wisdom from you that it will take to lead us. May our governor and our state legislators not only hear from you but welcome your voice as you call out to them regarding their need for personal salvation.

May the spirit of wisdom be given to our Supreme Court justices and the Congress, as well. I pray for Mexico that the many peoples there in such poverty will have opportunities to hear a plain presentation of the Gospel as we have here. For the countries of Central America I ask that you would . . . (You can keep on filling in the blanks here.)

I also ask, dear Father, that you would Open the doors of Opportunity to those ministering in your name—political doors and personal spiritual doors. As Jesus said, 'No one can come to me unless the Father who sent me draws him'" (John 6:44). In Jesus' name, Amen.

I am not so naïve as to think that these short suggested exercises in focusing our prayers will be all that is needed for us to mature in prayer. I am hoping, however, that as you use them, these methods will grow into a skill that you will become so adept at using that you will automatically fall back on them. That is how habits are formed and as we look back over our lives don't we want to see ourselves in the habit of praying? I pray that they will become a way of constantly turning your mind towards prayer and following the Scriptural admonition to "Pray without ceasing" (1 Thessalonians 5:17).

As we share these subject outlines for prayer with each other we can be more accustomed to "thinking God's thoughts after Him" as someone has said. I pray that something as simple as these ABC's of prayer can become a way of truly broadening our prayer horizons and focusing our intercessory efforts both private and corporate. May God bless you in the effort. I am confident that He will.

7

MORE ACCOUNTS OF GOSPEL PRESENTATIONS

I'm sure you will agree with me that some of the most uplifting experiences you have had are when you have heard someone share how they finally felt the need for God's forgiveness and came to faith in Christ. It is as they share their own faith journey from doubt, confusion and guilt to a new world of abundant life in Christ that we tend to relive our own conversion experience and enjoy it all over again. Those are times when we may also come to realize that we have a new partner in Kingdom business. It just feels good to hear that someone else is now on their way to heaven with you, doesn't it? That's why I will now recount for you a sampling of many more seekers who have gone from being pre-Christians to those who have experienced the new birth. I'll group them by topic—sort of.

OUT OF THE BLUE:

In sharing the stories of other people I will be brief. I would love to flesh out the characters but I feel the need to give only the necessary details since some people I've talked with over the years may not want to be identified. I have lived in the same small city now for nearly 22 years so I'm just trying to protect their privacy.

These out-of-the-blue kinds of occasions really reinforce the need to be "Always Ready." Let me tell you about "Cindy," who wheeled up to me in her wheel chair one morning as I was doing some paper work in the lobby of her building. I was sitting on a sofa concentrating on my charting for that day when she rolled up and said, "Chaplain, can you tell me how I can know for sure that I'm going to heaven? I'm on hospice care now and I don't really know what's coming for me."

Those are the kinds of experiences that either strike terror in the heart of the unprepared or joyful anticipation in the heart of the prepared. In another context some have jokingly said, "I was born ready." Not for this they weren't. Christian friend, that's why I am writing this important book, to help you *GET* ready so that your response will always be one of joyful anticipation. As a side note here, I do believe that God tends to steer the seeking pre-Christian to those who are always ready.

I began asking her questions about her spiritual readiness and it wasn't long before we were bowing our heads as I led her to pray out loud phrase by phrase after me while the busy lobby of passers-by came and went, oblivious to what had just transpired in her heart, in my heart and in Heaven's courts with the rejoicing of the angels.

One Sunday morning years ago when I was pastoring a church, I did something I only did occasionally. I felt led at the close of the message to ask if there were any people who wanted to make an appointment with me for later that week so we could talk about how they could know for sure they were going to heaven and three hands simultaneously just shot up. I jotted down the names. Monday morning I made phone calls to make appointments and during the week I met each of them in their homes. By the next Sunday all three had experienced the new birth.

One was a young man who worked as an automotive mechanic in a local shop, another was a middle aged woman who worked as a bookkeeper and the third was an elderly lady whose funeral I conducted a few years later. What was so interesting was that in my visits with them, all three said in nearly identical words, "I didn't raise my hand, you know. It just went up all by itself." The bookkeeper has since retired and we keep up now and then, remaining good friends. The mechanic and I bump into each other now and then, too, always with big smiles! Doesn't that make you want to be always ready? I surely do hope so.

FAMILIES TOGETHER:

Seeing family members pray together has been a special treat for me to experience over the years. I recall my time with "Rick" and "Becky" a father and daughter who both prayed to accept God's forgiveness as a gift after I took the time to explain to them how God's forgiveness doesn't work so they could grasp how it does work. It was just a few weeks later that I baptized them both.

In July of 1995 there was a couple I met with after the wife came to me saying that her husband didn't know the Lord as Savior yet and would I come to their home for a visit to help answer his many questions. He was expressing interest. That told me that he was beginning to feel the need for forgiveness, the all important first step. While she had been a Christian for years, his form of Christianity might best be described as "limited to having been born into it and then choosing to be done with it." I vividly recall sitting around their dining room table explaining to them how God forgives differently than we do. "Ken" was just so ready to pour out his heart to the Lord that it encouraged his wife "Eve" to do the same as she came back to a more vibrant relationship with Jesus. It's been a joy for me and others to see his life count for Christ at his workplace over the years since then.

Just a few months later they introduced me to their friends "Don" and "Linda." Neither of them had ever attended church much or experienced the Lord's forgiveness. Once again it was so great to see their faces and later their lives change as Christ entered in. Their high school aged daughter turned Jesus down, however, and in the intervening years have led this family through much grief. So we continue to pray.

OUT OF TRAGEDY:

Many times tragic events lead people to come to the end of themselves and finally turn to Christ. One such was a staff member in one of my buildings who had experienced three deaths of family and close friends in a nine month period of time. After the second death she came to me about her struggles with the grieving process. We prayed together; she received some help and she went on with her life. After the third death in her family she came to me, took me into an office, closed the door, turned to me and with pleading eyes and voice said, "I just can't do this anymore. I can't deal with all these deaths when I know I'm not ready to die myself. What do I do? Please help me!"

Oh, how ready she was--finally. Yes, she accepted a pen from me and forgiveness from God. It was stunning to see the miraculous change in her attitudes after that. It was a delightful privilege for me soon after that to attend the service in her church where she was baptized at the end of Sunday morning worship.

I simply must tell you the story of "Robin," too. Here is an example of natural consequences following sinful actions that God still uses to bring about some good. When I met her "Robin" was a middle aged woman who had ruined her life, her health and her relationships through her abuse of street drugs and beverage alcohol. One night while driving drunk and high on drugs, she ran a railroad crossing, was hit by a train and left barely alive. Because of a spinal cord injury she lost the use of both arms and both legs. She was also unable to move herself in bed, not even to squirm, and was totally unable to speak. Her only way of communication was with her eyes. She could blink and move her eyes to look from side to side a bit but she could not move her head much at all. As I began to get acquainted with her I offered to pray for her and she agreed to let me do that. The staff had instructed me that one blink meant "Yes" and two blinks meant "No." Because a chaplain always has to gain permission from the patient before praying with them, I always asked and she would always grant permission.

As the weeks went by I was so frustrated about how I might possibly bring her to faith in Christ. One day God just seemed to tell me that she was ready and it was time to launch "the conversation". (Remember my earlier discussion of praying for alertness to God?) Since many of the questions I ask people (see list in chapter eight) can be answered "Yes" or "No," I began. I'll have to admit, this was new territory for me but as I explained things to her I could tell that while her body was pretty much non-responsive, her mind and spirit were fully engaged.

Yes, she did pray to accept God's offer of forgiveness and as she did a crooked sort of half-smile broke out on her otherwise expressionless face. In just a few months she expired but there was no intention on her family's part to have a memorial service. I was really disappointed about that because I had wanted to share her testimony with them. Wouldn't that have been an exciting time for them to hear of God's great loving offer!

I can't wait to tell you about "Tess." because hers is such a great story. She was a caregiver at one of the buildings where I had worked for many years. She just wasn't feeling very well at all but since she only had a week or ten days to go before retirement she waited until then to go see her doctor. Just a couple of days after she retired I was carrying the hospital beeper in my additional role as occasional on-call hospital chaplain to cover for the chaplain when she is out of town when I got a message to come.

When I arrived the staff told me there was a lady who had come in through the ER who asked for me by name and wouldn't see anyone else. I went to her room and there was "Tess." She was in pretty rough shape. Her doctor had discovered that she had breast cancer that had already spread to her kidneys and the bones in her spine and the outlook was not only grim but very short lived, literally. She was in a panic and wanted me to pray for her but she was in such a state that I knew she wasn't ready to think clearly enough to work her way through a gospel presentation and absorb the whole story. But I prayed for her right then, asking God to tell her how much He loved her.

When I went back the next day I said, "I think it's time for us to talk about what's really important. What do you think?" She agreed, and in about 15 minutes or so she was ready to pour her heart out to God, first asking God to forgive her of all her sins and then thanking Him that he just did. She gripped the pen tightly—it was hers and so was God's forgiveness. In a few days she was stabilized and returned to the facility where she'd worked her entire adult life, but this time as a patient to receive care from her co-workers until she died.

Now here's where it gets really good. She began to share with her close care giver friends about what had happened to her in the hospital when she and I had prayed. She showed them the pen and tried to make the message plain but she didn't have the energy, the training or the experience to do all that she wanted to do. The authenticity of her experience came through loud and clear to her friends, though.

"Carrie," one of her staff friends came to me and said, "Ron, I want one of those pens, too." We both knew what she meant. Before we could get together for a visit "Tess" expired. A few days later we had a memorial service for her at the facility and I counted about 85 staff people and a few family members in attendance. There were people standing around the edge of the dining room when seating was full. I knew it was my opportunity to share the "rest of the story," as Paul Harvey used to say on his radio program.

I took plenty of time to do it and used some caregivers who were sitting in the front row as examples of how forgiveness works and doesn't work as I shared the illustrations of borrowed money. I did everything but give an altar call, so to speak. Interest was high; the people were tracking me well. It was a great experience of seeing people's faces as they thought long and hard about this new way of understanding God's forgiveness.

Within a few days "Carrie" and I were able to get together in an empty resident room and she too accepted Christ as Savior through tears and smiles. I see her now and then and she always greets me with a warm smile. Just the other day she told me that she has found a time to have her daily private worship time. Because she works almost every Sunday she can't attend church. Just today (I'm giving this volume a third reading.) I saw her in the hall and she held up the pen I'd given her as she said, "See, I'm using my pen!"

The part of the story that has yet to be told concerns "Doris," another staff member who was at that memorial service. She had also just received news that she had cancer and would be starting chemotherapy soon. She has always been a private person and she won't talk about her own needs. I approached the administrator in that facility as to the best way to be available to her; he said that she doesn't want to talk about it and not to make the first move. How my heart breaks whenever I see her now and then as she wears a scarf to cover her hair loss. I pray that she'll see that her greatest need isn't about her hair—or even the cancer—but about her relationship with Jesus—about feeling the need for God's forgiveness, etc.

"Debbie" contacted me because I had conducted a funeral for her family some years before and now that her husband left her she was ready for spiritual help. Because of her background as a Jehovah's Witness it took a bit of time for her to embrace the truth of Christ as a substitute sacrifice for our sin but as the Scriptures sank in she was ready and in January of 1999 she prayed through to faith in Him. It wasn't long before she lined me up with a visit with her cousin and she, too, came to faith in Christ as did her daughter.

"Karl" is another example of coming to faith from tragedy to triumph. He was high on street drugs when he had a high speed crash, wrapping his motorcycle around a tree. In that instant he was left a total quadriplegic and his wife and daughter were left to care for themselves. After I met him I continued to return for weekly visits. I do remember one time when he was especially distressed to see me leave his room. He cried out, "Please stay. Do you have to go yet?"

On one of those visits he was finally ready to admit that he'd surely sinned enough to keep him out of heaven. Before that he was one of many who just don't think that what they have done is quite enough to exclude them from entering heaven. I knew that there was no reason to push him because I have learned from experience that unless a person is convinced of that initial fact they aren't ready for any more information. He finally did pray to receive Christ on one of our visits. One of his first requests was for me to pray for his mother, which we have done frequently over the months.

"Dirk" was a hard working self-made cowboy type whose wife was a very faithful attendee at the church I was pastoring many years ago. He never was the least bit interested in church, although he was a wonderful family man who loved his children and doted on his grandchildren. He was a few years away from retirement when his doctor told him he had throat and larynx cancer. The doctor went on to explain that the surgery would be very invasive, leaving "Dirk" with a long-term open neck wound and the inability to ever speak again. He would also be on a feeding tube because of his inability to swallow.

His wife soon called to tell me that he was finally ready to talk about spiritual things before he went in for surgery. I remember sitting with him alone at the kitchen table while his wife made herself scarce so we could work through this alone. With the sound of traffic rushing by on the highway just outside their house, his heart grew quiet, surrendering all to Christ.

This was way before I began to give away unique pens, but the Bible truth, "for it is by grace you have been saved, through faith—and this not from yourselves, it is the gift of God—not by works, so that no one can boast" (Ephesians 2:8-9) became clear to him that day. As I used other illustrations of how God's forgiveness works and doesn't work I soon found myself sitting next to a changed man. God had truly met his deepest spiritual need. In fact, that's how I had opened the conversation--by asking, "What's God talking to you about right now?" I've used that question many times over the years especially when dealing with people who respond to an altar call at church or camp.

Within a few weeks he had surgery. The post-surgical pain and wound care were crushingly brutal. Palm Sunday was a few weeks after surgery and as usual his wife was in attendance at church. Because of his post-surgical needs he wasn't yet able to attend. Everything changed for that family on that day when I saw her son drive up to the church just after the close of the service to tell me that Dad had taken his own life that morning while Mom was in church.

Whatever your feelings are about suicide, I doubt any of us could have truly understood the pain and panic that was going through his mind at the time he chose the ultimate permanent solution to a temporary problem. Some of you may be thinking to yourself, "Ron, you're just letting him off the hook too easily." Wait a minute, what makes you think that I'm in charge of who is "on the hook?" I'm quite content to let God handle these kinds of cases. Didn't Abraham ask the rhetorical question, "Will not the judge of all the earth do right" (Genesis 18:25)? The understood answer is, "Of course He will."

"Rose" had a 21-year-old son fall asleep at the wheel and die in a car crash early one morning as he was driving to work. His live-in girlfriend was pregnant so there was plenty of grief to go around. When "Rose" and her husband met with me before the funeral I could tell that they could really benefit from some follow up visits so I offered to meet with them now and then.

I came to their house every two weeks for a number of months and took them through some of the grief recovery material I had developed when I was a guest lecturer at a hospital in the city where I had pastored years earlier. In time both of them came to accept Christ as personal Savior; they both have pens today. I rarely see her anymore but I know I'll see them both in heaven one day.

LAST MINUTE DECISIONS:

Some people may discount deathbed conversions but Jesus didn't when he saw the faith of the penitent thief on the cross right next to him. I'm sure that criminal thought that nothing good could possibly come out of the day of his execution. I'm also sure that when the day was over he was so glad that he ended up caught, convicted and crucified right next to Jesus. Here are some examples of last minute decisions I've seen people make. You've already heard of "Mel" and "Tess." Let me add another.

"Doug" was a tough old logger who had a friend attending the church where I was pastoring at the time. In the course of time I made an appointment to come to his home. While there I found myself answering questions, asking questions and explaining the way of faith. I explained to him that there are three kinds of faith—mental assent to the truth, faith for life's situations and faith for forgiveness.

It took a couple of visits but soon he prayed so eagerly to accept what Jesus did on the cross as good enough. He realized that he no longer needed to feel obligated to God to find a way to make up for his life of sin. He was elated, so much so, that when I returned to their home the following week to begin the discipleship process he asked, "Now preacher, what do you call what happened to me last week?" I told him that Jesus called it being born again. His response? "Well I didn't know what to call it. All I know is it's the best damned thing that's ever happened to me!"

Not surprisingly, he remained a bit rough around the edges until the day he died. Some months later I was privileged to conduct his memorial service and share his story about coming to Christ for forgiveness. At the close of the service one of his sons came up to me and asked to make an appointment to talk about his own spiritual needs. Needless to say he was finally ready and he, too, prayed to accept Christ. Isn't that great?

There is a lady in town who did foot care for residents in the assisted living centers. We'd been friends for years because I had led her husband to faith as I sat with both of them around their kitchen table. She called one day to tell me that one of her patients was ready to talk about Jesus. She gave me his name, the name of the building where he lived and his room number. She pretty much expected me to be there within a day, two days at the most. I had gotten used to occasionally getting similar calls from her over the years. When I did, I knew that she had prepared the way and I would most likely find a hungry seeker. She served for years as my "advance man," so to speak. She's been a true missionary.

I gladly went and we chatted but the gentleman wasn't ready to get serious yet. I made an appointment for the next week and began to pray in earnest. Surely you can believe that I used the prayer outline I've explained above. When I returned the next week he was very ready. After I went through my presentation and he was holding his new pen, he prayed so sweetly for God's forgiveness and "sealed the deal" by thanking God for already forgiving him. I went back the following week to see him for his first follow up visit and he'd expired the day before. Go figure. God knew.

"Mavis" is another one, but in a different way. I was able to pray with her to receive Christ before Alzheimer's got to where it is now. Today we are not able to have these kinds of conversations because of her increasing dementia and loss of mental acuity so I'm glad the Lord opened her heart in time. She tells me that she is so fortunate because her parents live just across the street. Of course they've been gone for many years.

"Nina" also is an Alzheimer's patient with whom I was able to pray. Her husband came to me pleading with me to come "make sure she's going to heaven." (Do you see what I mean about God bringing seekers to one who is always ready?) We made an appointment for a few days later and during that time we both prayed that she would be lucid enough to really be able to understand enough to accept God's forgiveness.

What do you suppose? According to the staff she had the best hour she'd had in months—the hour we were there. I purposely kept my presentation short and in about 10 minutes or so she was ready to pray and thank God for the gift of His grace. Her husband ended up with the pen. Let me give you just a follow-up to their story. He ended up in the same building with her as his health failed and as I write this I was in the building earlier today only to find out that he had expired just a few hours before. Now they're both home with Jesus!

"Florence" was a resident in one of my buildings a few years ago. She had been watching her roommate's health steadily decline until she died. It was then that "Florence" came to me and said she wasn't sure if she was going to heaven or not and could I answer her questions. Of course I could and would and did! How sweet to hear her pray as she came to the place where she knew for sure she would be with Jesus!

A friend of a friend gave me a call a few years ago to tell me that she knew of a woman whose husband had just been diagnosed with kidney cancer and would I set some time aside to visit with them. I stuck with "Allen" for the weeks it took him to come to Christ and then the mere months it took him to die.

In another situation I walked into a building and began to make contact with those who were new admits since the previous week when I'd been there. "Elaine" was on the list. When I entered the room, her daughter "Sylvia" asked her mother if she wanted some private time with the chaplain. At first it seemed that Mom was going to put it off but "Sylvia" gently persisted and offered to leave the room so "Elaine" could feel free to bare her soul before the Lord with me. She soon prayed to receive God's gift of forgiveness through Christ. Her daughter was so relieved and thanked me profusely as I went on down the hall. Three days later Mom died. Yes, God does meet people "in the nick of time." Are you ready to lead a seeker to that next level? If you will be ready God just might send some seekers your way. Won't that be exciting!

AFTER LONG CULTIVATION:

I mentioned earlier about the lady who had been active in a Bible-believing church all her life but had not come to the place of experiencing the new birth. She is not alone in that. There are many others. Her are examples of a few of those.

"Tina" had her caregiver call me asking for a home visit. I'd been acquainted with her for a number of years and assumed that she was a Christian from our brief encounters. In spite of being a quadriplegic she made it to church with a friend now and then. Something was bothering her that day and I didn't know what it could be but I've learned that when someone calls for me it's usually to talk about their personal relationship with the Lord Jesus. Usually they are just not sure that when they die they will go to heaven. This situation was as I suspected. That's why I had my wife pray for me as I went. I also asked Janice to pray for "Tina" in those five areas of spiritual need most common to pre-Christians.

As I stood next to her bed in her apartment she began to share that she had serious doubts about whether she was really headed for heaven. As I asked probing questions it became apparent that once again the problem was that she thought that God forgives us the same way we try to forgive each other. Deep in her heart she knew those were unsuccessful endeavors. All her life she'd been in a great church but the concept of grace hadn't found a home in her heart.

When I got to the place where I offered her a pen it was a bit awkward because her hands don't work well enough to grasp anything firmly. In fact, when she did have it in her hand she couldn't feel it. She did get the message, though, and was eager to pray, honestly thanking God that her sins were forgiven.

"Carol" had MS; she was another severely disabled person both in body and in spirit. Her paralysis was nearly total. As I slowly worked my way through these important concepts she just seemed to eagerly drink it all in. When I was finished I used another of my favorite concluding questions—"Does that make sense?" That's another cue I learned from the "Evangelism Explosion" training. If it doesn't make sense you want to know here before you go on to prayer. Just ask and if necessary go over some item that they don't understand too clearly. Sometimes we Christians get so eager to pray with somebody that we "pick green fruit," so to speak.

She replied that it did make sense but she was taking no chances and wanted to be doubly sure so would I please start at the very beginning, leave nothing out and go through it all again. She was not pressed for time and I've learned not to be either. After another 20 minutes or so she was finally ready to pray and joyfully accepted God's forgiveness as a gift.

Over 20 years ago I met "Elmer" through the local car club of which I was a charter member. I not only have enjoyed the classic car restoration hobby over the years but have purposefully used my friendships as opportunities to share the gospel message with many pre-Christians in the collector car hobby. Over the years I had been in "Elmer's" home, his garage and his barn looking at cars and talking about cars.

I remember a time a few years after we first met when he stood in my garage and I asked him if he knew for sure that when he died that he'd go to heaven. He wasn't and he didn't want to talk about it either. Some ten years went by during which we kept up our friendship—even trading cars. He got my old Thunderbird and I got his old Chevy.

More years went by. Parkinson's disease began to rob him of his mobility and dementia took a toll on his wife of over fifty years. He had to move to one care facility and she to another. During that time I once again approached him, asking him if he was ready to talk about his relationship with the Lord. He finally was ready to talk about it and when he was holding his new pen in his gnarled hand it finally made sense to him.

A number of months later his wife passed away and when I conducted a memorial for her at the building where she'd been living I heard their daughter talk about her own faith in Christ. After the service and during the refreshment time I took her aside to tell her about how I'd prayed with her dad some months earlier. The tears poured out in relief because she just wasn't sure about her dad's spiritual condition because he had always been a quiet, stern man. She and I have a special bond now as I meet her coming and going to see her dad. She calls me the brother she didn't get to have. Her dad comes to Bible study now and then as he can.

OUT OF A LIFE OF SIN:

I already told you of "Karl," the young man who had a motorcycle crash while driving under the influence and leaving him a total quadriplegic. And I also told you about "Robin" the lady who suffered horrible injuries from a train crash. Here are some other examples of how God has worked a total change in hearts that were far away from the Lord.

Many years ago we moved to pastor a different church. We weren't there long at all before I got a call from a man who had been on the administrative staff at the college from which Janice and I had both graduated nearly 20 years earlier. When he found out that I had just moved to the city where his grandson lived, he wanted me to contact that grandson and his wife to talk to them about knowing Jesus.

These young adults had become drug users and were in the process of ruining their lives. I called, told them of the connection and asked if I could come to visit. I mentioned that it was the wish of his concerned grandfather. "Jake" and "Sylvia" agreed to let me come to their house, which surprised me. So I quickly took them up on it and once again was excited in anticipation of seeing what God might do.

Sure enough, in about an hour total they were kneeling on the floor at their sofa, pouring their hearts out to God, asking for the forgiveness that only Christ could provide. When we got up from prayer I knew that God had thoroughly met their need and changed their hearts when two things happened: they asked when church started Sunday morning so they could be on time and they made plans for the next Saturday to take their stash of cocaine and drug use paraphernalia out to the desert and bury it all. Don't you suppose that the way in their hearts had been well prepared by the prayers of those grandparents? I think so, too.

"Jake" told me on Sunday that they buried the mirror on the top of their stash with the face up so that if they ever got tempted to go back to their old way of life they would see themselves coming and take a second thought. I called "Jake's" grandfather the next day. He and his wife were overcome at the power of the gospel. While we were there "Jake and "Sylvia" became very active in the church, doing all they could to serve the Lord.

"Richie" was a junior high age kid when I first met the family. As time went by, he got in with the wrong crowd and began ruining his life with street drugs. His mother asked me to keep praying for him, and of course I did. One day the opportunity finally came to share with him the explanation of how forgiveness from God does and doesn't work and he was ready to hear it. He was born again through the blood of Christ and left drug use behind altogether. The last I heard he was happily married.

"Jonathan" was a young man who had ruined his life with drugs so badly that his family refused to give him any more mulligans—no more "do-overs." Because he had taken advantage of the kindness of all his family members, his mother and his sisters now refused to let him come live with any of them anymore. I met him when he was in his late twenties or early thirties. He had recently been admitted to one of my physical rehab buildings because he was so sick.

I was able to get the phone number of one of his sisters--the one he said was "very religious." She and I agreed to seek God in prayer for the core spiritual needs of this young man. I agreed to talk to him about his relationship with Jesus the next week when I was back in that city. Yes, it was a brutal time, taking him through all the things in his life he needed to confess to God as sin. I listened as his repentance rang true and cried with him as he experienced God's complete forgiveness. I am glad to report that the staff, his sister and I were able to find him a placement with Teen Challenge that worked out great.

Stories like "Jonathan's" were repeated many times when I worked part-time in a hospital as a guest lecturer and personal counselor for residents in a 30-day alcohol and drug treatment center. Because it was a Catholic hospital I was given free rein by them to lead people to personal faith in Christ. In fact, they had recruited me for the job. That was a great year and a half as I saw many come to personal faith in Christ! I didn't count how many or keep a list of names of those who surrendered to Christ but He surely has that list in the "Lamb's Book of Life."

PRE-MARITAL COUNSELING:

Over the years of pastoral ministry I have made it a point to use pre-marital counseling sessions to build up to a gospel presentation on our fourth or fifth visit. Lots of couples have come to faith during these times. Here are a few of those stories.

"Valerie" had been a preschooler in a church when we first went there to pastor. Twenty years later she called and asked if I would do the wedding for her and her fiancé "Jack." When we got to the session when I deal with spiritual issues I asked each of them to write down answers to these questions: "Have you come to the place in your spiritual life where you know for sure that when you die you will go to heaven and be with Jesus? What list of reasons would you give Jesus as to why you think you should get to enter heaven?"

Their answers revealed that while she had made a profession of faith as a child he had not and neither of them was living a life of surrender to the Lord at the time. I worked my way through the presentation as you've seen above and sure enough they both prayed, he to become a Christian and she to come up to date with Christ.

That same thing has happened many times over these past forty years. Some situations have turned out better than others. One couple saw that after learning what I'd taught them in these sessions they had no business getting married and so they didn't. Years later she came to me with another choice of a groom that was a much better fit. Another couple I prayed with had tragedy strike when the bride expired of natural causes just a few years after they had been married. I was so glad that they both had prayed to receive Christ during our last session together.

SECOND CHANCES:

Technically speaking, every one of us gets a second chance to make better decisions every morning when we wake up to face a new day. What I'm talking about here, though, are situations in which I've met someone and talked to them about faith in Christ but they've turned it down because they weren't ready yet. Sometimes, though, we meet again and I have a chance to start the conversation over and this time they meet Christ not just me. Here is an example of what I mean.

I have already told you about "Elmer" my old car-guy friend who fits that description. Now let me tell you about Christopher, yes his real name. (I'll tell you why I'm using his real name in a bit.) He had been admitted to one of my buildings following leg amputation surgery. A mutual friend called, asking me to go see him and hopefully be able to lead him to faith in Christ. I went but he just wasn't ready. No amount of trying to gently guide the conversation piqued his interest in spiritual things. He was later discharged.

Some months went by when I noticed his name on the list of new admits again and felt a real thrill. I just knew God had brought him back for another "run at it." Unfortunately his other leg had to be amputated, too. He was understandably depressed. I met with him every week when I was in his building but spiritual openness was very slow in coming.

One day I was just getting started in a gospel presentation when we were interrupted by caregivers and I had to leave the room so they could change wound dressings. Another time a week later I was mid-way in explaining how forgiveness doesn't work when his wife called him on the phone; I left the room so he could talk to her. During the third visit, another week later, I was pumped, prayed up and doing my best to keep the devil at bay when we were able to get through it all, answer his questions, hear his prayer of confession and watch him accept God's forgiveness as a gift while he held his new pen in his hand. Oh, what joy there was in that room! Both of us were in tears.

That evening I called our mutual friend with the news and he was just overcome at the mercy of God. He said, "As quick as I get off the phone I'm going to go pray and thank God for answering my prayers!" Once again, you can see the essential link between prayer before hand and the response to a gospel presentation.

When I went back to see Christopher the next week I asked him if he knew the meaning of his name and he said, "I do; it means Christ-bearer." And then with a smile he said, "And now I am one, but more than just in name only!" Now you can see why I decided to use his real name.

I then decided that he would also be able to handle a more difficult line of questioning so I asked, "Did you ever think there would be any benefit to your losing that second leg and having to be here for another series of many weeks or months of physical therapy?" He quickly replied, "I didn't then but I sure do now. I lost both of my legs but I gained heaven. What a great trade!"

Here's another situation similar to Christopher's story. I also need to use his real name just because it fits so well. His name was John Calvin. I don't know if his family named him after the early Church reformer but they may have. At any rate John was admitted to one of my buildings after a heart attack and heart by-pass surgery. I tried to talk with him about spiritual things but he just wasn't very interested and I've learned not to push. He was discharged in a few weeks only to be readmitted several months later following a stroke. He was still able to speak and concentrate but more effort was required.

As time went on I became very well acquainted with his wife who prayed with me that he would "make his peace with God." One day several weeks after having been admitted this second time, I was sitting on the edge of his bed while he sat to my right in his wheel chair and Dorothy sat on a chair across from me and next to him. It was time to get serious in our conversations. It wasn't long before he was holding a new pen—*his* pen, and praying for God to take his guilt away.

His daughter, a Christian lady, flew out from Tennessee so she could talk to her dad about it in person. She asked, "Daddy, would it be okay if I was baptized with you?" Now if that doesn't get your tear ducts loosened up! That morning I baptized them both from a bowl of water the kitchen provided. When he expired a few months later his daughter called me from Tennessee asking, "Are you sure Daddy is in heaven?" I told her I was sure and she could be, too.

BROUGHT THROUGH OTHERS:

You've probably noticed as I've shared the accounts of peoples' lives throughout this book that many times people come to Christ because of the direct influence of someone else, usually a friend or family member. Here are a couple more instances of that same thing. From 1993-1997 there was a series of five friends or family members who came to Christ as the first influenced the second, the second influenced the third and so on.

"Zoe" came to Christ in September of '93. I distinctly remember sitting in her living room and explaining to her how she could know for absolute certainty that a home in heaven could be part of her future. Her husband was a small business owner in the city where we pastored at the time but I can't off hand remember just how I first came into contact with her. I do remember buying supplies from him in his store. Her husband never surrendered to Christ while I was there as pastor but her friend "Reba" did as did Reba's husband, "Everett." They in turn were an influence on another family member, "Sally" who was also influenced by a friend "Kathi." It took some years for all this to play out but what a joy to see it unfold. All of these folks are still following the Lord. Of course, there are still some others in the family circle who have yet to say, "Yes," to Christ, so we keep on praying.

In one of our congregations we had a family who had lived out in the country but moved in to town just a few blocks from where we lived. It was nice to have near neighbors who were also part of our church fellowship. "Eileen's" parents also lived in the same neighborhood not very far away. Her mother attended a church in town but "Eileen" was concerned for her dad's salvation because he had never made a personal profession of faith in Christ and wouldn't attend church either with his wife or his daughter. He was having some severe emotional problems at the time and was apparently not getting much help. I began spending some time with him and over the course of weeks he, too, accepted *a* gift from me and *the* gift from the Lord.

"Nora," a nurse in one of my buildings, was always such an evangelist, too. She was always so concerned about her patients' spiritual welfare. "Sam" was one of those. She said to me one day when I came to her building, "Ron, I think 'Sam' is ready for you to talk to him straight up about coming to Christ." She was right. Within minutes it was obvious how hungry he was for real soul satisfaction. He, too, received a pen from me and then peace with God. After he was discharged "Joyce," another caregiver in the same facility urged me to follow up with a home visit and I was able to do that twice. What a pleasure to see the joy of Christ on his face!

"Donald" was another of "Nora's" projects. He had been in her building for years but declining health had required a hospital stay again and this time his prognosis on his return was not good. As soon as I entered her building that day she quickly came to me and said, "Ron, would you come with me right now to pray for 'Donald?' I'm afraid we may not have him many more days."

I assured her that's exactly what I wanted to do. He was weak but not so weak that he couldn't understand how deep his need of God's forgiveness was. With "Nora" standing at my elbow, he prayed so sweetly as he held his new pen in his hand which was gnarled by arthritis. In just a couple of days he went home to see Jesus and how glad both "Nora" and I were that God had us there in the nick of time.

MISCELLANEOUS STORIES:

"Teresita," a Latina housekeeper who was raised Catholic was such an encouragement to me. One time as I was standing in the doorway to her supply closet and just chatting with her, she turned to me and said, "Being a chaplain must be hard sometimes." As I talked with her about helping people come to accepting God's forgiveness before they die she said, "The only way to peace with God is through confession of sin. I know that only God can forgive; the priest just listens in." I thought, how right on! In that regard my ministry has just been as a guide and listener. God forgives; I just listen.

"Eileen's" roommate had just expired a few days earlier and she was still mulling many things over in her mind about her own lack of readiness to die. When I got to her room she brought up the subject; she wanted to know for sure that she was going to heaven so I began to ask questions to guide her through the process and soon she, too, held a new pen in her hand and a new relationship with God in her heart.

"James's" Parkinson's disease had brought him down to the point of barely being able to swallow or speak. Some months earlier "Gloria," his charge nurse, who was a wonderful Christian lady, had asked me to go check on him because he had been down to her station talking about wanting to know God better. As I visited with him I confirmed that he was already born again, ready to meet God and just had a heart for more of God. Isn't that the way it's supposed to be?

Anyway, he was also a Catholic who figured out on his own that the Church didn't provide salvation, Christ did all that for us on the cross and we just need to come to the place where we see how much we need to be forgiven and accept God's forgiveness as a gift. I thought, "Right on; he's got it."

Then in his whisper-thin soft voice he slowly and deliberately shared a gem with me. I had to lean over his bed to hear him softly say, "I know now that the old statement that it's not the destination but the journey that's important is just backwards—the destination is what's most important; the journey is nothing."

A pretty courageous thing to say seeing as how his disease-ravaged body was basically keeping him prisoner until Jesus comes for him. Why does he linger? I don't know; I don't presume to speak for God. I do know that all the disease, destruction and death we have in this world is the result of the fall of mankind into rebellion and sin first expressed in the Garden of Eden and then in every human heart along the way.

I also am confident in the Scripture's promises that all of that will be swept away and everything will become new.

NOT ALL GET "FIXED:"

I mentioned earlier about how some folks were not yet feeling the need for God's forgiveness and therefore have yet to seek him. Some may even take the pen as a gift from me but aren't yet accepting the gracious gift of forgiveness from the Lord who loves them so much. Here are some accounts of those kinds of situations. As I recount these I am also mindful that things can change. Out of these folks there may yet come some who will surrender to Christ.

I remember sitting with "Darryl" at our dining room table explaining to him how this all works. He went from being a typical pagan American teen to being a Mormon when his Mormon girlfriend took him on as a project. He had pretty much made a mess of his life, but now he was a self-made man--a very successful businessman and civic leader in his fifties. He also became a leader in that religion in every way until he became disillusioned about their finances and their forcefulness.

When we got down to the end of the presentation he said he was just not ready to "go that far." As we chatted I suggested that perhaps it was his pride that was keeping him from surrendering to God over this issue and he readily agreed, "I'm just not ready to humble myself to God. I'll figure this out on my own somehow." He left our home, drove away and I haven't heard from him since, even though I've emailed him. I know I can't push; he has to come to the end of himself, so we'll just continue to pray.

"Erny" was a patient in one of my buildings about an hour's drive from the city where we live. I met his sister when she had come out from Minnesota for a visit. She asked if I'd continue to visit her brother and I assured her that I would. When I got the word that I only had a few weeks of employment left with the company I decided that it was time to get "terminally earnest" with "Erny."

I started by asking him my opener questions: "Are you sure you're ready?" and "What would you say?" I went through the explanation of how God's forgiveness is different from ours and so forth. He did understand the issue and the solution but kept dodging when I pressed him. I explained to him that the next week when I would be in his building would be the last time I'd be there in that city as an employee availble to talk to him about his relationship with the Lord.

All week long I lifted him in prayer using the outline as I've explained earlier in this book. When I came to him that next Tuesday I asked him, "So, 'Erny,' have you been thinking about what we were talking about last week when I was with you? Are you wanting to know for sure that your sins are forgiven?" He responded, "Well, that's easy for you to say!" and went on to tell me that it was harder for him to believe than it was for other people.

I knew we were in for trouble; I tried to work around it but in just a moment he asked, "Is it raining outside?" I got the message; that was his way of ending the conversation on that topic for good. It was with a heavy heart that I trudged across the parking lot to my car, bowed my head over the steering wheel and wept, asking God to bring someone else into his life who will be there at the right time to harvest a crop from the seeds that had been planted.

"Veronique", a French lady, actually in the same building as "Erny" is such a sweetie. Her sparkling blue eyes, white hair and French accented English make it a delight to sit and visit with her. Once when I asked her if she had come to the place in her spiritual life where she knew for sure that when she died she'd go to heaven she replied that she wasn't sure at all. When I asked her if she wanted to be sure I fully expected to have her say that she did want to know. Her answer floored me, however, when she said, "No, I don't think so." I have never had anyone reply that way in over forty years. I tried to gently pry around the edges in the following weeks but all to no avail.

"Mary Jane," a nurse in a different building, said that she had "tried being a Christian but it didn't work." Now she is into "Reiki," a form of Buddhism, and is "just so happy." Another heartache for sure.

"Roy," a high school classmate of one of my cousins was in his 60's with Parkinson's and a resident of one of my buildings. I spoke to him at least three or four different times about knowing his sins were forgiven but without any positive response from him. He always put me off. He finally expired after being in that facility for well over a year.

"Kari" is maybe one of my greatest heartaches. She's a nurse for whom I have prayed for years. When I first began to work in her building she first introduced herself to me as the facility's pagan lesbian and I should "just get used to it." Because I could notice a little twinkle in her eye when she said it I knew I was being set up but in a friendly way. I was just sure she said it to find out how I would react. I was very careful not to be reactionary and just roll with the punches, so to speak. I think she wanted to first see if I could take a punch before she trusted me with anything personal.

I told her on many occasions that if she ever wondered if God loved her she just needed to remember that what Jesus did on the cross for us all was the greatest proof of God's love for us. There were a few times she let me pray for her, her partner or her children from a heterosexual marriage that had ended in a painful divorce. We prayed a few times in her office and another time while we stood at the copy machine right out in the dining room with lots of people around. Now and then she would even casually introduce me to someone as her "Pastor." Many times it seemed as if she was just so close to saying, "OK, Ron, give me the whole story." But that moment never came. Yes, that's been sort of a downer for me, but you probably have similar circumstances, too. She remains on my everyday prayer list.

Let's remember that these friends and acquaintances of ours are not permanently locked in to their present spiritual condition. They can still respond to the love of Christ reaching out to them. I am sure you remember when I encouraged you earlier in this book to recognize the need in your own life for endurance and to ask God to provide it. Well, it's that time, isn't it? Let's keep on keeping on as we continue to pray that these dear ones will feel the need for God's forgiveness as their greatest need, that they will understand the concept of God's grace as a gift, that the Holy Spirit would remove hindrances to the Gospel in their lives, that they would ignore the idols in their inverted value system and that they would realize that judgment for sin is sure and certain unless they entrust themselves to Christ.

8

A SAMPLER OF QUESTIONS

I include here a sample list of some of the questions I have used over the years. Feel free to use whatever you can, but please don't feel like they are intended to be used all at once on any one person. Get familiar with them so they easily come to mind when needed. Notice that many of them do tend to logically come together as a group and follow a logical line of thought. Feel free to develop your own questions, too, of course. But the goal is to be *ALWAYS READY!* I anticipate that these questions may actually cause some readers to ask more questions so I've interspersed some comments that may help to answer some of your questions about these questions.

1.   Isn't it great to know that God loves us?

This is frequently my first question. Notice that they will be hard pressed to answer "No." Are they going to say, "No, it is not so good to know that God loves me"? If they question whether God does love them, that's okay; that's a subject you can handle. Sometimes a person will say, "If God really loved me things would be going better." I gently remind them that circumstances are not a reliable way for us to measure God's love by giving them this illustration: "Suppose you had a young child who came home from school one day and told you that he learned that you didn't love him anymore." In answer to your questions he would let you know that since he had had a really bad day at school that was proof that you no longer loved him. Actually that's when you would probably express your love in even greater warmth. Having a bad day, month or year only proves the temporary nature of our physical existence, not the love of an eternal God. Of course the greatest proof of God's love is what Jesus did for us all on the cross and it's appropriate to remind them of that.

2. Would it be okay if I asked you some questions about your spiritual life?

It really is important to gain permission to enter this level of conversation. If they are not ready it will be fruitless to force the issue prematurely.

3. Would you consider yourself a Christian?

Ask it this way. Don't say, "Do you think you're a Christian?" This sounds too harsh, doesn't it? It almost sounds like you are presenting yourself as an adversary. You can also just skip this question and go directly to question four. I often do.

4. How did you become a Christian?

Don't skip this one. Their answer here will tell you volumes about their view of God and their relationship with Him. How would you respond if they say, "I've always been a Christian?" Think about it ahead of time because you will hear it some time for sure. Since becoming a Christian is a decision each person must make for themselves that assumes that you were faced with that decision sometime in the past. Get them to talk about it if you can.

5. Have you come to the place in your spiritual life where you know for sure and certain that if you were to die today you would go to heaven and be with Jesus or are you still just hoping?

Notice that I gave them two options to choose from. That take's the pressure of having to say, "No." They still can say "Yes" to something.

6. Wouldn't it be great if you could go to bed tonight knowing that?

Here, you are giving them a chance to express a positive sentiment about the prospects of knowing Christ.

7. Suppose you were to stand before God and He would ask you for a list of reasons why you should get to be in Heaven, what would you say?

You might have to back up and probe a bit but don't go on until they talk about their list. If they still hesitate to talk about it you might suggest that they think about how the average person would answer that question and they will most likely come up with a list. Then you can ask them if these items express their own personal feelings. Do you see how that indirect approach can be much less threatening?

8. Have you come to know the Lord as personal Savior yet or are you still on the way?

Notice that once again I gave them two choices, not a yes or no. At least they can say they are still on the way.

9. How close are you to knowing Jesus as Savior?

No matter how they answer the previous question this one can still reveal a lot about their mindset.

10. How far away were you when you started this process?

Once again, notice that words have meanings. This question assumes that they are aware that they made the decision at some time to get started and it further assumes that it is a process; it is okay for it to take some time. On one occasion I discovered that the person to whom I was talking indicated by outstretched fingers the answer to question nine but outstretched arms to the answer to question ten. I said, "You've come a long way already, haven't you? Are you ready to go on to the next level?" By the way, that person did pray to receive Christ that day. That was the guy at the parade in Portland that I mentioned above.

11. What has helped or hindered you so far?

There are hidden dangers in this question. Answers here may reveal a lot about family history, etc. Try to keep it to spiritual issues if possible. You don't want it to turn into a time of blaming others for their own decisions.

12. Would you like for me to share with you how I came to know for certain that I have eternal life?

I use this one sparingly.

13. Do you often feel separated from God? Why do you suppose that is?

Note the use of the word "often." If you leave it out the question becomes greatly changed. You are also asking them to evaluate themselves. It's better if they see themselves and the causes of their spiritual needs without too much outside input if possible.

14. What is it that separates people from God?

The answer you're looking for is "sin." Don't let sins become synonymous with mistakes in your use of the two words. They are vastly different. We look back to see our mistakes; we look forward to make decisions to obey or to disobey God—that makes it a sin.

15. Do you think you have sinned enough to keep you out of heaven?

I may only use just a few of the questions in this extensive list but if there is any hesitation on the part of the person with whom I'm speaking, this will always be one of them. Don't be afraid to use it. It's pretty hard to come back to it later, although I have at times. If someone still feels that he has not yet sinned enough to separate them from God you will need to review some things, won't you? It may be helpful if you take them through the Ten Commandments and have them note how many they have broken.

16. Have you ever felt the need for God's forgiveness?

This is what we've been praying for, isn't it?

17. Have you ever asked Him to forgive you?

Sometimes I hear, "Every night." That's why the next question is so important to follow up with.

18. Do you know for sure that He did?

This follows up question five doesn't it?

19. Would you like to know how God forgives differently than we forgive each other?

This usually piques their interest. Many times I'll explain that most people aren't sure if God has forgiven them because they are confused about how God forgives. We think He forgives us the way we try to forgive each other. See discussion in chapter five.

20. Have you ever felt like your faith in God is too weak to work?

Here is where you can explain that faith isn't something that we work at doing as much as it is selective surrendering. See question twenty two below for a further discussion of this topic.

21. How does that make you feel to know that God's forgiveness is a gift?

Of course this would follow your discussion of that subject. I had a man say to me, "If it's a gift then I won't have it. I've always made my own way and I'm not going to change now." No amount of explaining or probing could get him past this point of pride. At least when I left, we both knew the issue. Remember, everyone "doesn't get fixed."

22. Did you know that there are three different kinds of faith in God?

I often explain that there is the mental assent kind of faith to believe the facts of the Bible about Jesus dying on the cross for our sins, second there is the kind of faith to trust God for help in life's situations and then finally the kind of faith for forgiveness of our sins. The last kind requires that we let go of everything else and completely fall back on Jesus, like "falling off a log."

23. Does this make sense?

This is an extremely important question to conclude with. You want to know here if you need to go back to cover something in more detail or just repeat it to help them understand. They aren't ready to surrender to Christ if it doesn't make sense. That's been the problem all along so take your time.

24. What part is unclear?

Be sure to listen as they tell you. Let them finish explaining before you jump back in.

25. Would you like to receive God's forgiveness as a gift right now?

You can see why it's imperative to be sure to include the words, "right now."

26. Why does it seem hard for some people to accept God's forgiveness as a gift?

I use this question when a person seems hesitant. Wording it this way isn't as "in your face" as saying "Why is this so hard for you?"

27. Could I lead you in a prayer to God that you could repeat after me out loud phrase by phrase?

Be sure to include the words, "repeat after me," "out loud" and "phrase by phrase." Repeating after you takes the pressure off them to spontaneously come up with something to say at this most important time in their life. Regarding the matter of praying out loud, do remember the words of Paul, "The word is near you; it is in your mouth and in your heart, that is the work of faith we are proclaiming: that if you confess with your mouth, 'Jesus is Lord,' and believe in your heart that God raised him from the dead, you will be saved. For it is with your heart that you believe and are justified, and it is with your mouth that you confess and are saved" (Romans 10:8-10). If people tell me they don't want to pray out loud because they are embarrassed I pretty much insist that they speak to God not just ponder about their spiritual need. I may read these verses to them at this point. I've learned over the years that this is just so important. This is a hurdle they must get over. When they do, I've always seen such freedom and joy just beaming from their facial expression.

28. Now that you've prayed, how does it feel to know that you are forgiven by God?

This is just one more follow up, giving them a chance to verbalize their experience.

29. Would Jesus lie to you about any of this?

Aren't rhetorical questions fun? You may recognize this one from The Four Spiritual Laws *from Campus Crusade for Christ fame.*

APPENDIX 1
IF GOD CAN USE A DONKEY

Our son Brian was our pastor for a few years over a decade ago. I was so impressed with a sermon he preached on July 23, 2000 that I kept the notes I had taken that Sunday. I include them here as a useful tool to inform, encourage, train and motivate us all to stay involved in the ministry of personal outreach. Because I couldn't have said it better myself I won't elaborate on his notes or try to preach the sermon again for you. You can quite easily follow along. I think you will agree with me that this Scriptural account can be a real encouragement to all who want to be *always ready*.

IF GOD CAN USE A DONKEY
GOD CAN USE ME, TOO!
(Numbers 22:21-34)

<u>What do I need to DO to be an effective witness?</u>
1. I NEED A SENSITIVE SPIRIT TO SEE GOD.
"The donkey saw the angel of the Lord" (Numbers 22:23).
2. I NEED TO BE WILLING TO ENDURE HARDSHIP.
"Balaam beat her" (Numbers 22:23).
"So he beat her again" (Numbers 22:25).
"He beat her with his staff" (Numbers 22:27).
3. I NEED TO SPEAK.
"Then the Lord opened the donkey's mouth, and she said to Balaam, 'What have I done to make you beat me these three times'" (Numbers 22:28).
"Whenever you are arrested and brought to trial, do not worry beforehand about what to say. Just say whatever is given you at the time, for it is not you speaking, but the Holy Spirit" (Mark 13:11).

4. I NEED TO LIVE A LIFE OF INTEGRITY.

"Have I been in the habit of doing this to you" (Numbers 22:30).

<u>What do I need to KNOW to be an effective witness?</u>

1. KNOW THAT GOD'S GRACE WILL BE WORKING.

"Then the Lord opened Balaam's eyes and he saw the angel of the Lord standing in the road with his sword drawn. So he bowed low and fell facedown" (Numbers 22:31).

2. KNOW THE DESTINATION OF THE UNBELIEVER.

"The angel of the Lord asked him, 'Why have you beaten your donkey these three times? I have come here to oppose you because your path is a reckless one before me'" (Numbers 22:32).

3. KNOW OUR IMPORTANT RESPONSIBILITY.

"The donkey saw me and turned away from me these three times. If she had not turned away, I would certainly have killed you by now, but I would have spared her" (Numbers 22:33).

APPENDIX 2
A VOICE FROM ETERNITY

One of those people who received Christ back in the mid 1990's sent me a poem shortly after she received the joy of forgiven sin. I saved it and am including it here even though neither of us has been able to find out who authored it. All internet searches list it as "Author Unknown." If you find out do let me know.

"A VOICE FROM ETERNITY--
YOU FORGOT MY SOUL"

You lived next door to me for years;
We shared our dreams, our joys, our tears;
A friend to me you were indeed—
A friend who helped me when in need.
My faith in you was strong and sure;
We had such trust as should endure.
No spats between us ever rose;
Our friends were alike, also our foes.
What sadness, then, my friend, to find
That after all, you weren't so kind.
The day my life on earth did end
I found you weren't a faithful friend. . .
For all those years we spent on earth
You never talked of second birth.
You never spoke of my lost soul
And of the Christ who'd make me whole.
I plead today from hell's cruel fire
And tell you now my last desire.
You cannot do a thing for me;

No words today my bonds will free.
But do not err, my friend, again;
Do all you can for souls of men.
Plead with them now quite earnestly
Lest they be cast in hell with me.

APPENDIX 3
SHOWERS OF BLESSING

While the topics for prayer listed above are for the specific *spiritual* needs of Christians, pre-Christians and intercession for the world at large, it is also appropriate for us to pray for the other needs we face in life as well. Here is a simple but effective way I've used to keep my prayers varied but still specific. I'd like to think that if we are praying for ourselves and for each other in these seven areas that will pretty much cover everything. See if you don't agree. Once again I have used a simple memory tool—this time it is an acrostic of the word SHOWERS. You may be acquainted with the old Gospel song entitled *Showers of Blessing;* what you might not know is that the phrase comes from the Bible, "I will bless them and the places surrounding my hill. I will send down showers in season; there will be showers of blessings" (Ezekiel 34:26). What a great promise from God! I will also use Scriptural examples once again as our guide in how to pray and what to pray for in these areas of life.

§AFETY: "While I was with them, I protected them and kept them safe by that name you gave me" (John 17:12). These words of Jesus as he spoke to his father give us a clue to how determined he was to protect his disciples and keep them safe in every way, both physically and spiritually. I would think that would give us the clue that it is fine for us to continue to pray for each and ourselves this same way.

HEALING: "Dear friend, I pray that you may enjoy good health and that all may go well with you, even as your soul is getting along well" (3 John 2). If the "disciple whom Jesus loved" was concerned enough for his friends to pray for their physical health, then we can, too.

OCCUPATIONAL NEEDS: "Make it your ambition to lead a quiet life, to mind your own business and to work with your hands, just as we told you" (1 Thessalonians 4:11). Perhaps there are people who are unemployed or under employed for whom we can pray more specifically.

<u>W</u>ISDOM: "For the Lord gives wisdom, and from his mouth come knowledge and understanding" (Proverbs 2:6). "If any of you lacks wisdom, he should ask God, who gives generously to all without finding fault, and it will be given to him" (James 1:5). How many times we go to a friend for advice and counsel before we bring the need to the Lord! Let's follow the Scriptural example and bring that need to God.

<u>E</u>DUCATIONAL: "Fathers, do not exasperate your children; instead, bring them up in the training and instruction of the Lord" (Ephesians 6:4). "Train a child in the way he should go, and when he is old he will not turn from it" (Proverbs 22:6). We can pray that our family members will do well in school and that their teachers will feel the need for God's forgiveness. We can easily include broader educational needs of our family as well, perhaps making a concerted effort to listen to the Lord's direction about which college to attend, for instance.

<u>R</u>ELATIONSHIPS: "For if you forgive men when they sin against you, your heavenly Father will also forgive you. But if you do not forgive men their sins, your Father will not forgive your sins" (Matthew 6:14-15). These words of Jesus surely do emphasize the need for us to keep our relationships with each other in good order so we stay in good fellowship with Him. I can also heartily suggest a reading of Matthew 18:15-17 to see Jesus' expanded instructions on how to maintain good relationships.

<u>S</u>PIRITUAL: "In those days John the Baptist came preaching, 'A voice of one calling in the desert, "Prepare the way for the Lord, make straight paths for him."'" (Matthew 3:1, 3). Notice that John's ministry was to prepare the way for the coming of the Lord into the lives of the individuals who were listening to him. In a certain sense, this embodies all of the fifteen prayer topics about spiritual needs covered in earlier chapters, doesn't it?

So, there you have it, seven simple steps to help guide, focus and intensify your prayer life through every type of need you may have. Of course, all of these helps are like new tools—of no value unless they get used. So give them a try. My goal isn't just that you be informed, or even moved, but that you would be changed.

AFTERWORD

After the years of ministry, the months of gathering these stories and the many weeks of writing them down I still find myself with no place to stop sharing how God has been at work in peoples' lives. That is because nearly every day brings something new.

Just last night, a Friday, "Joyce," one of the caregivers from my building across the street walked over to our house (Most of the day shift staff members in that building know where we live.) to ask me to be sure to come back soon to talk to two men she was especially concerned about. "Ray" was actively dying and not able to speak very well. She prayed with him and asked him to squeeze her hand if he wanted to ask Jesus to forgive his sins. He squeezed her hand and "Joyce" prayed with him.

"Steve" is another matter. In a matter of just three years this troubled man lost his mother, father, house, dog and pickup, then fell and broke his hip (No, it's not a country and western song). He told "Joyce" he wanted me to come back for a longer visit. I had seen him on Wednesday but only briefly.

Jump ahead with me; now it is Saturday. I just got back from the facility to find that "Ray" had died in the night after "Joyce" had prayed with him and "Steve" talked about lots of things but as I gently questioned him I could tell that he didn't feel the need for God's forgiveness—yet.

So "the beat goes on," so to speak. For "Steve" it's time to go back to the beginning and pray that he would feel the need for God's forgiveness greater than all of his other needs, that he would begin to understand that because of God's grace, forgiveness can only be a gift, that the Holy Spirit would remove the hindrances to that in his life, that he would be willing to ignore the idols in his life and understand that judgment for sin is sure and certain after we die unless we accept God's forgiveness on His terms.

It's on days like this that I feel like I can't stop writing. How can I bundle this volume up and send it off to the publisher just yet. Then I remember that the Acts of the Apostles ends in similar fashion—with the understanding that there will never be an ending place in Kingdom ministry for any of us until the return of the King. May the Lord bless your efforts with the joy of seeing many faces brighten and lives change as people receive God's gift of forgiveness.

STOP THE PRESSES! I've always wanted to say that but now I have a good reason. This book just came back to me for some final editing changes before going to print so I have a chance to add a paragraph or two.

Do you remember "Gordon" and "Betty," the couple I mentioned in chapter five? They were the ones who had never felt the need for God's forgiveness so I just kept on praying for them every morning for some eighteen years. Very recently I got a phone call from "Betty" saying that "Gordon" had been diagnosed with cancer and the prognosis was not good. She asked if we could get together soon. Her words to me were, "We've talked about it and we just need to get right with God."

It took a few days for both our schedules to clear so we could keep an appointment. But things changed rapidly when I got a call from the hospital chaplain in a few days that someone had been admitted through the ER and he wanted to talk with me. It was "Gordon." We met in the hospital and with a fresh spiritual hunger they both just lapped up my words about how God's forgiveness doesn't work and how it does work. When "Gordon" received his pen he burst into tears and said, "I didn't know it was this easy!" His wife also prayed that morning to receive God's forgiveness as a gift.

I spent some time with the two of them at their home after that but just about ten days later he expired. In the days leading up to that, I said, "Gordon," soon we will be having a memorial service for you. What do you want me to tell your friends?" His reply through labored breathing and with great effort was, "Tell them I wish I would have done this a lifetime ago." That's exactly what I did as I told them that

I thought that the most important words we could hear from someone would be his dying words.

Because he was so involved in our city's business community and in some charitable organizations, his service was attended by over five hundred people. Only a small minority were Christians. I shared how he had come to a personal relationship with Christ through accepting the gift of forgiveness and let the group know that if anyone there wanted to get together with me to talk about their own spiritual needs I would be glad to make myself available. Pray with me that there will continue to be a harvest from the planting of those gospel seeds.

And the beat goes on.

CPSIA information can be obtained at www.ICGtesting.com
Printed in the USA
BVOW021035160512

290271BV00001B/6/P